What to Do When You're
Cranky & Blue

a guide for kids

James J. Crist, Ph.D.

free spirit
PUBLISHING®

Library of Congress Cataloging-in-Publication Data
Crist, James J.
    What to do when you're cranky & blue : a guide for kids / James J. Crist, Ph.D.
        pages cm
    Includes index.
    ISBN-13: 978-1-57542-430-9
    ISBN-10: 1-57542-430-4
1. Depression in children—Popular works. 2. Depression in adolescence—Popular works. 3. Self-management (Psychology) for teenagers. I. Title.
    RJ506.D4C7495 2014
    618.92'8527—dc23

                                                                        2013034680

eBook ISBN: 978-1-57542-641-9

The concepts, ideas, procedures, and suggestions contained in this book are not intended as a substitute for professional help or therapy.

Reading Level Grade 5; Interest Level Ages 9–13; Fountas & Pinnell Guided Reading Level T

Edited by Catherine Broberg and Eric Braun
Illustrated by Michael Chesworth
Cover design by Tasha Kenyon
Cover illustration © Bubble86 | Dreamstime.com
Interior design by Marieka Heinlen

10 9 8 7 6 5 4 3 2 1
Printed in the United States of America
S13970913

Free Spirit Publishing Inc.
Minneapolis, MN
(612) 338-2068
help4kids@freespirit.com
www.freespirit.com

Dedication

I dedicate this book to all the young people I've worked with who have struggled with cranky and blue feelings, or depression, and have learned to overcome them. I also dedicate it to my family members and friends who have dealt with depression. I admire your ability to keep going even at times when it seemed too much to bear.

Acknowledgments

I'd like to thank my editors, Cathy Broberg and Eric Braun, for their help in organizing the book and making it more readable. I'd like to thank Renee Burdett, M.D., for her help in understanding the medications used to treat depression and bipolar disorder in children. Thanks also to Vian Gredvig, M.S.W., L.I.C.S.W.; Thomas S. Greenspon, Ph.D.; and Ginger Venable for reading and commenting on the manuscript.

Contents

Introduction

This book is all about feeling grumpy, sad, or down—feelings that *all* kids have sometimes. Who wouldn't feel cranky or blue if their best friend moved away, or if they were being teased or bullied in school? But this doesn't mean the feelings are easy to handle, especially on your own. And that's partly why I wrote this book.

I'm a psychologist, and I've talked with many kids who had problems with grumpy, sad, and lonely feelings. They told me how their feelings made it hard for them to eat, sleep, or get along with people at home and at school. I helped these kids better understand what's going on in their lives and find healthy ways to deal with their feelings. In this book, you'll learn about some of the ideas that worked for them.

But for some kids, feelings of crankiness and sadness go very deep. They may be grieving because a loved one died, or they may be trying to understand why their parents got a divorce. (*Grieving* means being really sad about a loss or a difficult event.) Feelings of sadness and loneliness that don't go away can be signs of grief.

They may also be symptoms of *depression*, an illness you'll learn more about in chapters 6 and 7. Depression is a serious problem for a growing number of kids today—another reason why I wrote this book. Whether you feel sad and alone some of the time, most of the time, or all of the time, this book can help.

In this book, you'll learn about the signs of being cranky or blue and what these feelings might be telling you. More important, you'll find out what you can do to help yourself feel better. You'll also discover ways to feel less down or lonely and more connected to other people in your life.

You don't have to handle grumpy, sad, or lonesome feelings all by yourself (in fact, it's much healthier to talk about them). I encourage you to read this book with someone at home who takes care of you: a family grown-up such as a parent or stepparent, a foster parent, a guardian, a grandparent, or an aunt or uncle. The "Note to Grown-Ups" on pages 113–120 offers tips for adults who take care of you. Be sure to show this special section to your adult helper.

You may also need the guidance of an adult who specializes in treating kids who have problems with feeling sad and lonely—for example a counselor, psychologist, child psychiatrist, social worker, therapist, or doctor. That may seem scary to think about, but experts like these can really help. If you're wondering what it's like to get counseling, see chapter 10.

There are many other people out there who can help you as well. You might talk to your teacher, an adult neighbor you trust, or someone at your place of worship. If you want, you can talk to people your own age, too.

Sneak Preview (What's Inside This Book)

Part 1 of *What to Do When You're Cranky & Blue* focuses on grumpy or "down" feelings that most kids have at one time or another.

- Chapter 1 discusses the big and small things that often make kids feel cranky, lonely, or "down in the dumps." It also talks about how different people react to these painful feelings.

- Chapter 2 has ten "Blues Busters," or coping skills you can try at home, at school, or anywhere else to help shake those sad feelings.

- Chapter 3 offers written exercises that can go deeper than the Blues Busters in helping you get a handle on your feelings.

- Chapter 4 is all about making—and keeping—friends. It includes ideas on choosing friends and describes the skills needed to be a good friend. Making connections with others is one of the best ways to get over the blues quicker.

Part 2 focuses on deeper feelings of sadness and loneliness—ones that are too hard to handle alone. If you have some of the problems described in chapters 5–9, please talk to a family adult right away. You may need the help of a counselor or doctor who can identify your problem and suggest solutions.

- Chapter 5 is about **grief**, a deep feeling of sadness that occurs when something terrible has happened in your life such as losing a loved one or a pet, or if other sudden changes have occurred.

- Chapter 6 talks about **depression**—when you feel cranky, blue, lonely, and unable to do much. (But the good news is you *can* do something about it.)

- Chapter 7 discusses a specific kind of depression known as **bipolar disorder**. Bipolar disorder makes you feel really up sometimes and really down at others (kind of like a roller coaster).

- Chapter 8 talks about some other big problems that can be connected to feelings of long-term unhappiness or depression. You'll learn about bullying, eating disorders, drug and alcohol use, and neglect and abuse, and find ways to get the right kind of help.

- Chapter 9 talks about feeling like you no longer want to live, also known as **suicidal feelings**. Even if you've felt this way for only a minute, it's important to talk to someone. If you feel this way now or have often wished you could die, please get some help right now. Talk to an adult you trust, and don't wait. For suicide hotlines, turn to page 103.

■ Chapter 10 describes what it's like to go to counseling. If you're having a very hard time getting over your cranky and blue feelings, or if you have problems that are too big to handle on your own, you'll learn how an expert can help.

It may help to know that many kids and adults have overcome their cranky, sad, or lonely feelings by using ideas like the ones in this book, and *you* can, too. It may take some practice, but it will be worth it.

I'd like to know how this book has helped you and how you're coping with your feelings. You can also write to me if you have questions or a problem that you don't know how to handle.

You can email me at help4kids@freespirit.com or send me a letter care of:

Free Spirit Publishing
217 Fifth Avenue North, Suite 200
Minneapolis, MN 55401-1299

Be sure to send me your address, so I can write back to you. I look forward to hearing from you!

Dr. James J. Crist

Part 1

Getting to Know Your Cranky and Blue Feelings

Chapter 1

What It's Like to Feel Cranky and Blue

Kareem, age eleven, feels lonely since his family moved to a new neighborhood. He can't find any kids around who are his age. At his old house, his best friend lived right across the street, so he always had someone to play action figures or ride bikes with. Now no one is around except his younger brother.

■ ■ ■

Charlotte, age ten, doesn't have friends at school anymore. The group of girls she always hung out with suddenly "dropped" her a few weeks ago. They won't talk to her in the halls and they ignore her on the bus. She can't figure out what she did wrong and she's feeling pretty low. Charlotte wonders if she should try to make new friends—but it seems so hard to do. And what if her new friends drop her, too? It hurts to be treated that way. So, she eats by herself in the cafeteria and watches while the other kids play at recess. She's just too sad to join in. And she comes home feeling cranky, which makes it hard to get along with her family.

Everyone feels cranky and blue sometimes. These feelings are a normal part of life for kids and grown-ups, but that doesn't mean they're easy to deal with. It can be hard to cheer up when you feel down. You wonder if you'll ever feel good again.

Lots of things can make you feel sad. Big changes—like moving to a new city or your parents getting divorced—can lead to many feelings, including sadness and loneliness. But other things can also bring you down, such as losing a favorite CD or fighting with a good friend. Maybe you feel sad because someone you care about is feeling blue or having other problems.

Sometimes when you're sad, you might also feel cranky. When you feel cranky, nothing seems to make you happy and every little thing seems to upset you. You might feel lonely, too. You might wish you could be around others—or feel like you

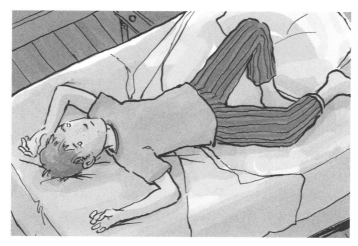

don't have anyone to be close to. If you're staying in your room and not coming out to play, you probably feel lonely. Sometimes, you can feel lonely even when you are around others. Suppose you're in the school lunchroom and other kids are having fun, but they aren't including you. Even sitting next to them, you might feel left out and alone.

Here are some things that often make kids feel sad, cranky, lonely, or blue.

Everyday things:

- not seeing enough of their mom or dad or others they care about

- being teased or bullied by other kids

- getting a bad grade on a test or an assignment

- having a disability that keeps them from doing things they want to do

- getting in a fight with a friend

- not making the basketball team or getting a part in the school play

- being bored

- gray and rainy weather

Big events:

- moving away from friends and family

- parents separating or getting divorced

- being mistreated by parents or other family grown-ups

- having a pet or family member die

Other times, kids—and grown-ups, too—feel sad without knowing why. You might wake up one day feeling blue, even though you can't think of a reason why. It's normal to feel this way from time to time. Usually, the sad feelings go away after a while.

How People Act When They're Blue

Not everyone acts the same when they're sad. Sometimes you can tell that people are sad just by looking at them. They may be crying, walking around with their head down, or avoiding other people. Other times, though, sadness 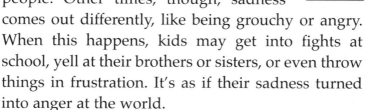 comes out differently, like being grouchy or angry. When this happens, kids may get into fights at school, yell at their brothers or sisters, or even throw things in frustration. It's as if their sadness turned into anger at the world.

Of course, you can have a mix of both. You can feel sad sometimes and grouchy other times.

Here are some typical signs of being sad or blue:

- You cry often during the day.

- You don't feel like playing games or joining in with other kids.

- You want to be alone a lot—at home, at school, or wherever.

- You don't seem to enjoy activities that you used to love (hobbies, games, sports, videos, and so on).

But feelings of sadness can also show up as feeling cranky or angry. For example:

- You might get mad or yell at people a lot, especially at home.

- You get into fights about little things you know don't really matter.

- You feel the urge to throw or break things— maybe you've even done this.

- Someone has told you that you're complaining or whining a lot.

Takeo's Story

Twelve-year-old Takeo has been upset ever since his dad moved to a different town. Now he only gets to see him every few weeks. He has started spending a lot of time in his room so he doesn't have to talk to anyone. Last night, when his mom knocked on his door and asked him to help with the dishes, he exploded and started yelling at her. The yelling got some of his angry feelings out, but he didn't feel good about being so mean to his mom.

Kids who are trying to be tough are more likely to show their sadness through anger. This is especially true for boys, because boys sometimes feel like they're being weak if they show their sad feelings. They may find it easier to get angry than to feel sad. In a way, feeling angry takes their minds off of being sad.

Some kids don't think they're sad or angry. They think they're fine and nothing's wrong. But sadness can show up as physical problems. This can include:

- headaches or stomachaches

- feeling tired, even when they've had enough sleep

- not being hungry or wanting to eat too much

These, too, can be signs of sadness. (Of course, they also can be signs of other physical problems, so it's a good idea to get a checkup with a healthcare professional if you're achy, tired, or in pain.)

Some Sadness Is Normal

We all feel "down in the dumps" sometimes. We have good and bad days. Maybe you've heard the saying that someone "got up on the wrong side of the bed." But for most kids, the feelings don't last. For example, if you feel sad and someone asks you to go outside and play, you might feel a little better. Once you get outdoors and move your body, you start to feel stronger and more energized. Playing with friends can get your mind off your troubles, make you laugh, and remind you that people care about you. And before you know it, the sadness has gone away (at least a little).

For things that are especially important to you, such as the death of a pet or loved one, you may feel sad for a long time. You may be able to go about your day as normal, but you just don't feel like yourself. You don't have as much energy as you used to and it's hard to get excited about new things. Usually, the more time that passes, the less sad you feel—and the less the sadness hurts.

Many people get the idea that sadness is "bad" or is something that should be avoided whenever possible. Sadness doesn't exactly feel *good*, but that doesn't mean it's bad. Plus, it can't be avoided—it's part of everyone's life.

If you feel sad a lot of the time, it may be a sign that you need some help. Feeling sad can tell you that you're learning how to handle a loss in your life. Sadness is part of the healing process. Feeling sad can also tell you that you need to work on fixing a problem. That problem might be making new friends, working harder in school to bring up your grades, or learning how to deal with bullies or an annoying sister or brother. The good news is, you can fix the problems in your life. Reading this book is a good start!

As you begin thinking about your feelings of sadness and crankiness, it may help to keep a journal. A journal is simply a private place to keep track of your feelings and thoughts. It doesn't have to be anything fancy and you don't have to tell anyone that you're keeping a journal. Use it to write about what's going on in your life, or draw pictures if that's more your style. Taking the time to write down your thoughts often helps you discover more about how you feel—and helps you think of ways to work through your problems.

■ ■ ■

You may also find it helpful to talk to other people in your family about what it's like to feel cranky or blue. What makes them feel this way? How do they work through their feelings? Talk to your adult helper, your brother or sister, or anyone else you trust. You'll learn more about journals and talking to others about sadness in the next chapter, Blues Busters.

Note: If your sad feelings make it hard for you to do things you like or need to do—like going to school, playing with friends, doing your chores, eating—they may be turning into depression. Go to chapter 6 to learn more.

Chapter 2

Blues Busters

Imagine you wake up one morning feeling horrible. Your nose is running, you're coughing a lot, and you feel kind of hot. You could go to school anyway, but you wouldn't have a good day. You know having a cold or the flu just takes time to go away. But getting plenty of rest, drinking a lot of fluids, and sometimes taking medicine can help you feel better faster.

Feeling cranky and blue is like having a bad cold. The feelings will probably go away at some point even if you don't do anything different, but there are things you can do to help yourself feel better faster.

This chapter describes ten of those things. I call them **"Blues Busters"**—tips you can use to make yourself feel better when you're feeling down. They'll help you get moving forward again, so you don't miss out on the fun things in life. You can use them at other times, too. Think of them as ways to keep yourself healthy.

Using Blues Busters

You can use these Blues Busters at home, at school, or anywhere you feel cranky or blue. The strategies are numbered, but you don't have to use them in any order. Try as many of them as you like and see which ones work best. They're all designed to work together to help you become stronger and healthier.

#1: Talk It Out

Talking about your feelings helps in many ways. By talking about what's going on in your life, you can learn new things about why you feel the way you do. Talking also is a way of helping to work sad feelings out of your body. When you share your sad feelings with someone else, the feelings don't seem so heavy and you don't feel so alone anymore. Most kids feel relieved after they get their feelings out. Others feel more energized.

A note about the Blues Busters: The more you practice them, the easier it will be to use them when you need them the most. Be sure to have fun with each skill, because the more fun you have, the more you'll want to practice—and that means better results!

If you're not used to talking about your feelings, it may seem strange at first. But with practice it will get easier.

Ask a family grown-up or other adult you trust if he or she has time to listen. Or ask a friend if you want. Here are some ideas for getting the words out:

- "I've been feeling pretty down lately. Do you have time to talk about it?"

- "Mom, I've been having trouble making new friends. Did you ever have problems like this?"

- "I was wondering if you could help me figure out how to handle some sad feelings."

- "Dad, this is hard for me to talk about, but I'm really sad about something and I want to tell you about it."

When you're talking to your adult helper, you can ask the person for ideas on what to do or you can ask the person to just listen. Either way is fine. Of course, other people often have new ideas that can be really helpful.

#2: Express Yourself

Everyone has lots of feelings. Some make us feel good and some bring us down. It's good to express your feelings, especially those that leave you feeling sad or lonely. That means letting your feelings out, or showing or telling others how you feel. You can talk it out, like in Blues Buster #1, or you also can use your creativity to express yourself. Here are some ideas:

- **Write in your journal.** (See page 14 for ideas about starting a journal.) The process of writing can help you figure out things—why you're angry with your best friend, how you can tackle a big project in school, or how you really feel about a problem. Writing also can help you release your feelings or make them go away.

- **Draw a picture.** Draw what you're sad about, or draw a picture that shows how you wish things could be. You can draw in your journal, if you want, or explore the possibilities with other art supplies—paints, chalk, crayons, or charcoal.

- **Make a collage.** Cut out pictures or words from magazines or catalogs that express how you feel. Then glue them on a sheet of paper or posterboard.

- **Make up a song or poem.** You can make it rhyme if you want, but it doesn't have to.

- **Play a musical instrument.** Play a song that reflects your mood, or make up one of your own.

Why is it so important to let out your feelings? Because holding them inside or pretending they don't exist creates other problems. Scientists have discovered that keeping your feelings inside can actually make you sick. The stress that comes from bottling up your feelings can make it harder for your body to stay healthy. It can make it harder to sleep, cause you to eat too much or too little, or lead to anger outbursts.

Another idea is to draw about things you feel sad or mad about and then rip up the picture when you're done. Imagine that you are ripping up your sad or mad feelings when you're ripping the picture.

You don't have to be a writer or an artist to express yourself. These projects are not for a contest or for school—they're only for you. Of course, if you want to, you can share your creative expressions with people you care about.

#3: Rev Up Your Engines—Get Moving!

Exercise is one of the best ways to improve your mood. Some people call it a natural remedy. And it's true—when you exercise, your brain produces chemicals called *endorphins* that help you feel better.

The thought of exercising might seem like too much when you're feeling sad—you'd rather take a nap or watch TV. Start small. Tell yourself you're going to do the activity for five minutes. Once you start, you'll probably want to keep going. Another idea to help yourself get going is to set up an "exercise date" with a friend. If friends are waiting for you, you'll be more likely to get out and join them. Plus, exercising with others is usually more fun.

You don't have to exercise a lot for it to help. Just do as much as you can. Even twenty minutes a day can help improve your mood. Here are some activities you may want to try:

- Walk the dog.

- Run around the block.

Exercise safely:

- Start slowly and don't overdo it.

- Stretch your muscles after warming up. Doing this lowers your chances of pulling a muscle.

- Take a break if you have trouble catching your breath or if you feel pain during physical activity.

- Be sure to drink plenty of water, especially on hot days.

- Set up an obstacle course and have races with your friends or siblings.

- Play sports, such as volleyball, basketball, street hockey, football, lacrosse, or soccer.

- Skateboard or go inline skating.

- Go for a bike ride.

- Ride a scooter.

- Jump rope.

Once you start exercising, the next step is to make a habit of it. Meet a friend to shoot hoops every Tuesday after school, or take a walk with your family every night after dinner. Besides releasing negative feelings, exercise can improve your sleep, raise your confidence, and help you meet new friends.

#4: Watch What You Eat

Sometimes people's cranky and blue feelings show up in the way they eat. People who feel sad or depressed might do one of these not-so-helpful things: (1) skip meals because they feel too upset to eat, (2) overeat because they use food to get their mind off their sad feelings, or (3) reach for the junk food because they think it might help them feel better.

Eating too little or too much isn't healthy. The key to a healthy diet is *balance*. You need nutritious meals and snacks throughout the day. Eating a healthy, balanced diet—one that includes plenty of fruits and vegetables—is especially important at this time of your life. You still have a lot of growing to do, and your bones, muscles, and organs need healthy food to develop properly.

A balanced diet also helps you feel stronger and more energetic—something that's even more important when you're feeling down. Feeling sad can make your brain and body feel worn out. At times like that, you need more strength and energy. That's where healthy foods come in.

Junk foods like chips, donuts, and candy aren't healthy, so try to avoid snacking on them too often. It's okay to eat them once in a while, though. If you have questions about eating right, talk to a family grown-up or ask your doctor, teacher, or school nurse for information.

Read chapter 8 to learn about problems with food called eating disorders.

#5: Focus on the Positive

When you're feeling down in the dumps, it's easy to see the bad side of things. The good news is that you can train your brain to see the brighter side, to be more positive.

Try this experiment: Look at this glass of water. Do you think the glass is half empty or half full?

If you thought it was half full, good thinking! You were focusing on what you *had* in the glass (water), instead of what you *didn't* have (empty space). This means you were looking at the glass in a *positive* way.

If you thought it was half empty, you were focusing on what you *didn't* have (more water), instead of what you *did* have. This means that you thought about the *negative* part of the glass.

To focus on the positive, try to think about what you DO have instead of what you DON'T have. Start by making a list of all the things you are grateful for. You can do this in your journal if you want.

For example, suppose you're sad or upset that you lost a spelling bee. Instead of feeling gloomy, you can challenge yourself to find the positives. In this case, some positives might be that you got to participate in a fun competition and even made some new friends. Of course, sometimes it's hard to find a positive, for example, when a pet dies. Instead of thinking about how sad you feel, try thinking of the good times you had together.

#6: Switch Your Brain Gears

Sometimes when something sad happens, you keep thinking about it over and over. But replaying the event or situation in your mind doesn't make it better and can actually make it worse. When this happens, you need to find a way to switch your brain gears and think about something else for a while.

Counselors sometimes call this "distraction," and it works for grown-ups, too! Here are some ways you can get your brain to switch gears:

- Read a book.

- Listen to uplifting music.

- Watch a funny movie.

- Play a video game.

- Try a new hobby, such as collecting baseball cards, scrapbooking, or photography.

If all else fails, go to bed! Often things seem worse at the end of the day. After you get a good night's sleep, you may find it easier to focus on the positive things in your life. Think of sleep as a way of recharging your batteries. In the morning, you'll have more energy to handle your sad thoughts and feelings.

Warning! Watching TV and playing video games may seem like a good way to switch your brain gears when you're feeling down or lonely, but be careful not to spend too much time in front of a TV or computer, or on a cell phone or other device. This takes away time from being outside playing with friends or doing other things that get your mind and body moving.

#7: Make Connections

If you're lonely, work on a plan to fix it. The best way to fix loneliness is to make connections with others. For example, maybe you've been keeping to yourself a lot, spending all of your free time reading or doing stuff on the computer. If that's the case, you might want to see if there is a book club or computer group for young people in the area. Or you could form one of your own. Suppose you're in an after-school program and you usually use that time to do homework. Try joining in the program's group activities a few times a week (and finish your homework after dinner). These things may seem hard, especially if you're shy, but with practice it does get easier. You can do it!

Making connections can also help if you're depressed. See chapter 4 for more tips on connecting with other kids and making new friends.

#8: Let Yourself Feel Blue

Admitting you're sad and letting yourself feel really sad for a while actually can be one way to "beat the blues." The key to doing this, though, is to set a time limit. For example, if you're feeling down because someone stole your bike, give yourself permission to be really sad about what happened. You could tell yourself, "I'm going to let myself feel really sad today. Then tomorrow, I'm going to walk to the park." Or, "This afternoon I'm going to play sad music and cry on my bed, but at six o'clock I'm going to join my family for pizza."

> Some kids cry a lot for no reason. This can be a sign of depression. Read chapter 6 to find out more.

Believe it or not, crying may help, too. Crying removes toxic chemicals from your body, which makes you feel less tense and more calm. Most people find that they feel better after crying.

#9: Take Time for Yourself

Being sad about something can be stressful and tiring. When you feel worn down like this, you need to give yourself a break. Take some alone time to relax and unwind. Read a book, take a warm bath, play a video game, or go for a walk. Lie down on the grass and watch the clouds go by. Anything that's relaxing and takes your mind off what's bothering you can help.

This time is just about you. During this break, you don't have to share, you don't have to compromise, and you can do what you want. You don't have to make anyone else happy—just yourself!

Taking time out for yourself can also help you look at alone time in a more positive way. "Alone" doesn't have to mean lonely. Lots of people enjoy their alone time and look forward to it. Here are some ideas on how to make the most of your alone time:

Plan for it. Schedule some time for yourself and what you'll do during that time. By planning your alone time, you'll look forward to it. Maybe you'll read something for fun, go on the swings at the playground, or write in your journal.

Use it to recharge. Being around a lot of people can drain you of energy. Quiet time alone can relax and recharge you so that you'll be more ready to have fun with friends later. You can even unwind with some deep breathing exercises if you want. Find a quiet place, get comfortable, and then focus on your breathing for a while. Breathe in slowly, then slowly breathe out. Try to count to five with each inhale and exhale.

Enjoy it. Use your alone time for your favorite hobbies or interests. For example, if you love skateboarding, you can use your alone time to practice skateboard tricks or read magazines or websites about the sport.

Use the time for reflection. Sometimes, we get so busy that we don't have time to think about what happens to us each day and how we feel about those experiences. Spend some quiet time alone to help you stay connected with your thoughts and feelings. You can close your eyes and replay your day, or write about it in your journal.

Daydream. Make up stories, or imagine yourself doing all sorts of fun and exciting things. Daydreaming can help you get your mind off your problems, too. You can dream of being an astronaut, a movie star, or a famous musician!

#10: Help Someone

Sometimes, being around others is the last thing you feel like doing when you're sad. But helping someone else can take your mind off your troubles and make you feel better about yourself. Whether you lend a hand to a family member, a friend, or someone else in the community, giving to someone else in this way is almost sure to boost your mood. Here are some ideas:

- Help your younger brother or sister with homework.

- Offer to play a game with your brother or sister.

- Ask your parents or other family grown-ups if you can help make supper or clean the house.

- Clean up without being asked.

- Help a neighbor or relative with chores or errands (check with your dad or mom first).

- Volunteer to help others at your school or in your faith community.

■ ■ ■

Talk to your friends and family about the Blues Busters, and ask people to support you as you try these strategies. Talk to them about what you've learned or show them some of the creative ways you have expressed your feelings. Your family and friends might even want to try these activities with you!

Chapter 3

Going Further: Pencil and Paper Exercises

For some kids, using the Blues Busters from chapter 2 is enough to handle what's bothering them. But others may have stronger feelings of sadness and may need (or want) to go a bit further. In this chapter, you'll find pencil and paper exercises that have been helpful for the kids I've worked with. You can try these written activities yourself and see if they work for you, too.

Doing the Written Exercises

If you don't have one already, it's time to get an adult helper: someone you trust who can look over the exercises with you and help you when you need it. The written exercises may stir up feelings that are difficult to handle alone. Dealing with these feelings will be easier if you have an adult to guide and support you. If it isn't possible for a family grown-up to help, ask your teacher or your school counselor.

If at any time you realize that working on these exercises makes you feel *more* sad or lonely, then stop and take a break for as long as you need. Talk about your feelings with an adult you trust. When you're ready, you can begin again.

If you've already tried the journaling ideas on page 18, that's great! You can use the same journal for all of the exercises in this chapter. If you don't have a journal already, now is a good time to start one. If you choose not to use a journal, a pencil and paper or a computer will work, too.

Try to Write Each Day

There's something about putting pen to paper—or fingers to keyboard—that helps release feelings. See if you can get in the habit of writing each day. Do it first thing in the morning or before you go to bed each night. But don't write on just the sad days. Be sure to write about happy times as well. This way, you can remind yourself of happy times when you're feeling sad.

Don't worry about writing a lot. Even one or two sentences a day can help. You don't have to write complete sentences or worry about spelling. You can draw pictures if you don't feel like writing.

Here are some ideas for your journal:

 Make lists of things you want to do, such as working on new hobbies, setting up times to get together with friends, or figuring out a plan for a school project.

 Make a list of things that make you happy.

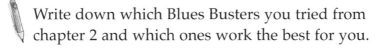

Write down which Blues Busters you tried from chapter 2 and which ones work the best for you.

Write about how you're taking care of your body. Are you exercising, eating right, and avoiding junk food? Is it helping?

Write about your grown-up helper and how that person is supporting you. Who else can you go to when you need help? You can write down phone numbers of people you can call.

List positive things you can tell yourself when you're feeling cranky and blue.

Get to Know Your Feelings

Before you can start getting over your sadness, it can help to learn more about your feelings. Writing about your feelings is a good way to sort them out and understand them better. Then, they won't seem so confusing and scary. Writing about your feelings will also help when you're trying to tell someone else what's going on with you.

Feelings can be positive or negative. They can also be mixed—positive and negative at the same time. For example, you can be excited about school ending but sad because you'll miss your friends over the summer. Whether your feelings are positive or negative or both, remember that they are never right or wrong—they just are.

Here are some common positive feelings:

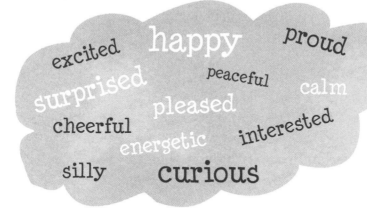

Make a list of the ones you have felt before, and add any other good feelings you sometimes have or would like to have more of. Then describe what kinds of things led to your feeling that way.

Now here are some negative feelings:

List which of these negative feelings you have had before, adding any others that made you feel down. Then describe what kinds of things led to your feeling that way.

Ask Others for Ideas

When you're trying to understand feelings better, sometimes it helps to talk to others. Ask different people you trust how they know what they're feeling—and how they make themselves feel better when they're feeling cranky or blue. You can ask your teachers, parents, older brothers or sisters, other relatives, counselors, and friends. Write down their ideas in your journal.

Create a Coping Plan

You can't predict everything that will happen to you during a day—or even what kind of mood you will wake up in. Still, it can be helpful to think about what kinds of things make you feel sad and create a plan to get through those feelings. Then, at times when you're feeling really low, you can look at your plan to remind yourself of what helps.

First, write down some things that might be sad for you. For example, your friends leave you out of their weekend plans, you get really sick and have to stay in bed for several days, or your dog runs away.

Next, make a list of things you can do to help yourself feel better. These are your **coping strategies**. (You can turn back to the Blues Busters described in chapter 2 for ideas.) If you know that some strategies work best for certain situations, be sure to mark that on your list. Otherwise, just list the things that have worked for you in the past or ideas you would like to try.

Keep the list of coping strategies in your journal or copy it onto a sheet of paper to hang in your room or locker. You could also use a stack of colored cards, with one strategy on each card. The next time you're feeling sad, look at your list and pick a few strategies to try. Try them one at a time until you start feeling better. You can put a checkmark next to a strategy each time it worked for you. This helps you figure out which ones work best. Don't be afraid to try a new idea—add it to your list!

Untwist Your Thinking

People often think things that happen *make* them feel a certain way. For example, "She made me angry" or "Spilling my lunch tray made me feel stupid." But this isn't how feelings work. Instead, it's what you *think* about what happened that causes you to feel a certain way. Looking at how thoughts and feelings are connected is called "the ABC model." It was developed by Dr. Albert Ellis, a well-known doctor who helped many people.

Here's how the ABC model works:

A = **A**ctual Event—something happens.

B = **B**elief about the event—what you believe the event means for you.

C = **C**onsequence (result) of your belief on your mood—you have a *feeling* about what happened.

A lot of people—kids and grown-ups—feel bad or make bad decisions because they aren't thinking clearly. The first step in "untwisting" your thinking is to take a good look at your belief about an event to see if there's another belief that makes more sense. If there is, you can try to replace your belief with a new one—and this can lead to more positive feelings.

Kiera's Story

Nine-year-old Kiera was working on her math homework at the dining room table when her older brother walked in and started yelling at her about the mess she'd made. He really let her have it. Kiera thought her brother hated her—why else would he get so upset just because she had spread out her homework on the table? She felt sad and deeply hurt.

But then Kiera tried to change her thinking, and she realized he probably didn't hate her. After all, she usually got along fine with her brother. Sometimes they even had fun together. Just last night they'd shared a big laugh together when their little brother got spaghetti sauce in his hair. Kiera decided something else must be bothering him. While this wasn't an okay way for her brother to react, her new thought did make her feel better. Her brother didn't hate her, and she didn't have to feel so sad.

Now you try it. Think of a time you felt sad after something happened. Then break down what happened.

Answer these questions:

A = What was the **A**ctual event?

B = What was my **B**elief about what happened?

C = What is the **C**onsequence of my belief on my mood?

Now, take a closer look at your belief. Does it make sense? Maybe you can *dispute* it. If you dispute your belief, you figure out that it isn't the best belief about what happened. You find another explanation for what happened. If you can, does the new explanation have an effect on your mood? Answer the following questions:

D = How can I **D**ispute my first belief with a new belief? (How did my belief change my mood?)

E = What's the **E**ffect of my new belief? What is my new feeling?

Sometimes it's very hard to untwist your thinking, especially if you're depressed. If you're having trouble using the ABC model, ask an adult to help you. A trusted grown-up's beliefs may help you dispute your own beliefs. A grown-up may be able to point out something you didn't see before.

Boost Your Self-esteem

Having high self-esteem means you feel good about yourself and think you can achieve your goals. When you do something well, you give yourself credit. When you fall short of a goal, you may be disappointed but you know it's not because something is wrong with you. It's just that things aren't always going to go your way. On days when you feel sad or lonely, though, it's natural for your self-esteem to drop a little. You might begin to wonder if people really care about you. You might believe you are to blame for all your problems. I call that twisted thinking, too.

Keeping a list of affirmations—good things about yourself—is one way to turn twisted thinking around. Start by listing three things you like about yourself. If you can't think of any, ask your family members or trusted friends. Or see if any of the ideas in the following list describe you, and start your list with them:

- I'm helpful.

- I'm kind.

- I'm funny.

- I get good grades in science.

- I'm good at sports.

- I'm a good reader.

- I try to cheer people up when they feel sad.

You can make your list as long as you like. Write your list in your journal and look back on it often, or hang your list in your room. If you put it near your bed, you can look at it first thing when you wake up and last thing before you go to bed. Each day, remind yourself of the good things about yourself.

■ ■ ■

Learning to deal with your sad feelings takes time and practice. Try working on these exercises every day—for as long as you can. The more you learn about your feelings and the more coping strategies you develop, the easier it will be to handle sad feelings when they come up. And then you can get back to the fun things in life!

Chapter 4

Connecting with Others: The Best Blues Buster

Juanita, age eleven, is down in the dumps since she moved the last time. Her mom is in the Army, so her family has to move a lot—it's just part of the job. But this time it was really hard for her to leave all of her friends. Moving seemed easier and even exciting when she was younger, but now it's just hard. She's afraid of making new friends because she knows that someday she'll have to say good-bye to them, too.

■ ■ ■

Twelve-year-old **Leroy** knows how Juanita feels. He, too, had to move, and he misses skateboarding with his old friends. But he realizes that the only way to feel better is to make new friends. He's good at football, so at recess he gets into a game. He tries to remember everyone's names, and uses them when he sees kids in the hallways at school. "Hey Jack, how's it going?" he says to one classmate. Before long, Leroy has a new group of friends. He still misses his old friends, but having new ones makes it less sad.

Having good friends can make life easier and more fun. With friends, you can be yourself, share your worries and fears, goof around, laugh, cry—you name it. It's healthy to share your world with other people. Besides being fun, others can perk you up when you're feeling cranky or blue. Friends can listen to you when you need to talk, and sometimes they have great ideas to help with problems. Sometimes you can help *them.* Helping out friends when they need it can make you feel good. Plus, when you get to know someone else, you discover more about yourself, too. You learn what you're good at . . . and what you're not.

Making Friends

Some kids seem naturally good at making friends. But anyone can learn how to make new friends and keep those friendships going strong. Just like learning to read is a skill that takes time and practice, making friends is also a skill you can learn and get better at. This chapter will show you how to get started.

Go Where the Kids Are

School is often the best place to make friends, since you're around other kids all day long. If you live in a neighborhood with lots of kids, you might find some friends there, too. Start by walking around your neighborhood, if it's okay with your adult caregivers. You might also be able to strike up friendships with kids in your faith community, at scouts, or in activities such as tae kwon do, soccer, or gymnastics.

You might make different friends for different settings. That's normal. For example, maybe you like to hang out with your neighbor on weekends, even though he is a few years younger than you. You might have a study partner for your Spanish class and a friend you like to play street hockey with. One person doesn't have to fill all of your friend needs, though lots of kids do find someone that they think of as their best friend.

Choose Friends

Once you find some kids, it might be hard to know which ones you want to become friends with. A lot of times you may need to be around people for a while before you can decide if you would be good friends. Watching how other kids play and treat their friends can help. You can also pay attention to what things they like doing. If you share some of their interests and they seem like nice kids, you may want to try to get to know them better.

Get Ready

Maybe you think it will be scary to approach other kids you want to be friends with. Feeling nervous at first is normal. Taking a few deep breaths might help calm yourself down.

You'll want to get into a positive mood before you reach out to new people. Remind yourself why you can be a good friend—make a list of positive things about yourself if that helps. (You can look back at the list you made from pages 38–39.)

It can also help to have positive body language when you're trying to connect with others. Your body language means what your body is "telling" others—the way you stand, sit, or position your arms. For example, suppose you're standing on the playground with your arms crossed and wearing a frown on your face. When other kids look at you, they may think you're not interested in being friends. They might not come up to you and invite you to play.

One way to improve your body language is to take a close look at it. You can begin by practicing saying hello in front of a mirror. Pay attention to how your face looks when you're doing this. Are you smiling? Are you frowning? Do you look scared? Try to smile and be as positive as possible. Tell yourself, "I can be a great friend."

Introduce Yourself

When you're ready, introduce yourself to other kids. You can say something like this:

You: Hi, my name's John. What's yours?

Peter: Peter.

You: Good to meet you, Peter.

Once you've met someone, and you've learned each other's names, the next step is to get to know each other better. Asking some basic questions is a good way to start. Here are some questions to help you get started:

What do you like to do for fun?

- Do you have any brothers or sisters?

- How long have you lived here?

- How do you like school?

Another fun question to ask starts with, "What's your favorite____?" You can fill in the blank with all sorts of things, such as:

- animal
- place to visit
- fun thing to do
- TV show
- movie
- video game
- book
- subject
- sport
- song

Being a Friend

Friendships take work. Friends give time and attention to their friends. The good news is that this is fun! When you like being around someone, you won't think it's work at all. Being kind, polite, and helpful are all good ways to be a friend. But there are lots of other things you can do to become the best friend you can be.

Be a Good Listener

Look people in the eye when you're talking to them. This lets them know you're paying attention to what they're saying. When your friends are talking, let them know you hear what they say and understand them. For example, if they're telling you something sad, you can say, "I'm sorry to hear that," or "That's sad." Don't interrupt or change the subject until they're finished.

Give Compliments

Giving compliments is a way of telling others that they're okay and that you like them. Watch your friends carefully and see if you can notice things they are good at or things you like about them. Then share what you've noticed. Be sure to be sincere—say only things that are true. Here are some examples:

- "Great job!"

- "Nice catch!"

- "I like your shirt."

- "You're a great help!"

- "Wow—you sure are good at this game!"

Say Thanks

You probably know you should say "thank you" when someone does something nice for you. Your mom or dad may remind you to thank adults, but it's also important to say thanks to your friends. You can thank them for helping you with your homework, for playing with you, for sharing their things, for teaching you a new skill, or for inviting you to play. It can be as simple as saying, "Thanks a lot!" or "That's really nice of you!"

Keep Your Word

Keeping your word means not breaking promises. It also means following through and doing what you say you're going to do, whenever possible. For example, suppose you have made plans to meet a friend at the library, but then someone else calls and invites you to the movies. Being a good friend means keeping your word and heading to the library, even if the movie sounds more fun. This can be tough at times! When you keep your word, your friends know they can trust you. It's a friendship skill. Remember the golden rule: treat others as you want to be treated.

Share and Take Turns

Sharing and taking turns are good manners that you probably learned when you were pretty young. But they're also good friendship skills that show others you care about them. There are lots of times you can practice these skills with your friends. For example, if you're eating some candy and your friend comes up to you, offer her a piece. Or you can share a magazine you are done reading.

Besides being a nice thing to do, taking turns when you're playing with friends can teach you new things. For example, your friend might know a basketball game or jump rope song you've never heard of. It might be hard to take turns when you're playing with a group of kids (because it takes longer to get a turn). Just do your best.

Be a Good Host

When friends come to your home, it's your job to make them feel comfortable. This way, they'll have fun and will want to come back. Maybe they'll invite you to their homes! Offer to take their coats when they arrive. Ask if they want something to drink. (Of course, check with your dad or mom first!) Introduce them to your family if they haven't met already. Give them the choice of what to play. If you decide to play a game, let your friend go first.

Be a Good Sport

It's natural to want to win when you're playing games or sports, but being a good friend means being a good sport. For example, if you win at a video game, don't get so excited that you make your friend feel worse about losing. Instead of bragging, say, "Nice game!" or "Good job!"

If you're playing sports, remember to give your teammates a chance to play. Don't "hog the ball." If some of your teammates aren't as good as the others, try to encourage them to do their best. Making fun of them for making mistakes isn't good sportsmanship. And it's not a way to make friends.

Handle Conflict

Even among best friends, conflicts sometimes happen. Maybe you and your friend want to do different things. Or you get into an argument over the rules of a game. Try to work it out so you can stay friends. Tell your friend how you're feeling. Ask your friend how he or she feels, too. You can say, "What can we do to solve this problem?" Staying friends is more important than getting your way or even being right sometimes. Be ready to compromise. (When people compromise, they both give up something so they both can get something.)

The best way to share your feelings is to start by saying "I feel" and then follow it with a feeling word, like *upset, hurt, sad, mad,* or *disappointed.* Explain what happened that

Of course, there are some things you shouldn't compromise on. If your friend wants to do something that's dangerous or against the rules, don't be afraid to say no. You can say, "I don't think that's a good idea." Or suggest a different idea.

led you to feel that way. Finally, say how you would like things to be different next time. Here's an example: "Li, I'm feeling pretty mad about what happened at school today. Those kids were making fun of my clothes and you just laughed with them. Next time I wish you would stick up for me." Don't forget to ask your friend how he or she feels, too.

Give Help and Support

You can also help others when they're feeling down or are struggling with something. This can be a great way to let your friends know you care—or even to make new friends. You can help with something simple, like holding open a door, or something bigger, like class work or punting a football.

If you see a friend looking sad, upset, or scared, ask what's wrong. Sometimes, kids want to be left alone when they're feeling down. Other kids may want you to try to cheer them up by telling a joke or getting them involved in something fun. Everyone is different. Be sure to ask what kind of help they want.

Get Help and Support

Friends can help you when you're feeling down, too. Calling a friend to get together when you're sad may be just the thing you need to feel better. You may want to talk to your friend about the problem, or maybe you just want to focus on having a good time and taking a break from whatever is making you sad.

You can also try asking a friend for help on your homework or a project you're working on. This can actually be a way of making your friendship better. Helping others makes people feel important and useful. The next time you're having trouble with your homework, try calling a friend and ask if he or she can explain it to you.

What Not to Do

Learning how to be a good friend takes a lot of practice. Don't worry—you'll get better at it as you go. Still, there are some sure ways to end a friendship. If you want to stay friends with someone, don't:

- tease

- criticize

- fight
- act bossy
- call your friend names
- talk about people behind their backs

Getting Help with Making Friends

If you've tried the ideas in this chapter and nothing seems to work, it's time to ask an adult for help. For example, you could ask your teacher or school counselor to watch you on the playground or in the school cafeteria where most kids learn to make new friends. Maybe they can tell you what you can do differently. Or they can pair you with other kids who, like you, are having trouble making new friends. Some school counselors will meet with small groups of kids during lunch to help them get to know each other. If you have a school counselor, ask him or her if this is something he or she can do with you.

■ ■ ■

If you're feeling sad or lonely, making new friends can be a great way to break out of your funk. If you already have good friends, let them cheer you up! Your friends are a great resource.

Part 2

Getting Help for Hard-to-Handle Problems

Chapter 5

When Someone Dies or Leaves You

(Grief)

Luis, age nine, is feeling sad and alone. His grandfather just died from cancer. They were very close and used to play checkers and watch movies at his grandfather's apartment every weekend. Now his grandfather is gone and he can't stop thinking about him.

■■■

Eleven-year-old **Sabina** misses her best friend, Olivia, who moved away a few months ago. Her new house is too far away to visit very often. Sabina has tried to make new friends, but no one can take Olivia's place. Even when she's with other friends, she still misses Olivia.

■■■

Luis and Sabina are coping with a feeling called grief. This strong feeling happens when someone you care about dies or leaves. You may also feel grief when something important in your life changes, so that you have to say good-bye to something familiar. The process of getting over such losses is called grieving.

Losses

Some losses, like when someone dies, are forever. We know that people who die won't be coming back. Maybe you have a grandparent, an uncle, a parent, or a friend who has died. As people get older, they often have more medical problems. Eventually, they die because their bodies can't fight the illness anymore. Sometimes, you know someone is going to die and you have time to say good-bye. Other times, people die suddenly, in car accidents or other tragic events. This can be especially hard to handle because it catches us by surprise. Even though it's very sad when someone dies, death is a normal part of life. Learning how to grieve for our loved ones who have died is part of growing up.

Not all kinds of grief involve someone dying. You can lose close relationships with people you care about in other ways as well. For example:

- A friend or parent moves far away.

- Someone close to you no longer wants to be friends anymore.

- You move into a new school or neighborhood.

- Your parents divorce and you no longer have your whole family living together.

These are all losses, too. If someone you love moves far away, you can't see her or him every day. You feel like something is missing in your everyday life. If you lose a friend, it can feel like having a hole in your heart.

Having a pet die is also very sad and may lead to feelings of grief. Your pet may have been a special companion and friend, and it's hard to know what your life will be like without this animal. It's normal to feel extremely sad and grieve when a pet dies.

Finally, you may need to grieve if you lose an object that was special to you. Maybe you have a stuffed animal or blanket that you always carried with you. One day, you lose it or someone takes it away. You no longer feel safe and secure. You can miss a stuffed animal or blanket almost as much as you can miss a person.

Everyone goes through grief at times. Sometimes it feels like grief will last forever. But the truth is that people who grieve do feel better in time.

Grieving

You may have many different feelings or reactions when a loss happens to you. The feelings may be stronger at first and then grow weaker as time passes. Or you may feel little at first, but then feelings come out later. Everyone handles grief differently. You may want to write down how you're feeling in your journal. This helps you keep track of how your feelings of grief change with time. Here are some common reactions to a loss:

- thinking it can't be true

- feeling sad all the time

- crying or sobbing

- avoiding things or places that remind you of the person, animal, or thing

- having strong feelings of wanting to be with the person or animal

- not being able to stop thinking about it

- not wanting to do much of anything

- being afraid that other loved ones will die or go away

- being afraid that you will die, too

People grieve in different ways. After a loved one dies, some people wear dark clothes and avoid doing fun things for many months. Others may light candles as a way of honoring the person. Some people celebrate the person's birthdays or other special anniversaries for many years.

Because grieving can be so hard, many people try not to think about it. They act as if nothing happened. This can make it harder for you. You may feel it's not okay to talk about the person or about what you're going through. But talking about your feelings of grief is very important. The more you talk about your feelings, and the earlier you talk about them, the easier it will be to get over your sadness. Here are some ideas to help you get the words out:

■ "I'd like to talk about all the feelings I'm having about Grandma dying."

■ "Mom, sometimes I feel very alone since Derek moved away. Can you help me with my feelings?"

■ "Dad, sometimes I don't understand why I still feel sad since Scruffy died. Is it okay if I talk to you about it?"

Stages of Grief

Many people who are grieving go through a set of stages. Knowing how the stages of grief work can help you better understand what you're going through. See if you can tell which stages you have gone through and which stage you're in now.

Denial—you pretend the loss didn't happen or you don't really believe it happened.
Anger—you're angry the person died or left you.

Bargaining—you think if you do the right things, the pain will go away or the loved one will come back. **Depression**—you feel terribly sad because of the loss. **Acceptance**—you accept that the loss happened and are ready to get on with your life.

Not everybody goes through all the stages, so don't worry if you skip one or if you go through them in a different order. Also, you can feel different things from different stages at the same time. Certain stages last longer for some people and shorter for others. It can take weeks, months, or longer to get through the grieving process.

If someone close to you has died, chances are your parents or other family grown-ups are also grieving. It can be hard and even scary to see a parent cry, especially if you've never seen grown-ups cry before. If you see family grown-ups crying, you can ask if they want a hug. But remember that it's not your responsibility to take care of your grieving mom or dad. They are adults and are responsible for taking care of you. Your family grown-ups may not give you as much attention as usual during this time. Try to be patient. If you need to talk about your feelings, though, be sure to tell them. Even if they are crying, most grown-ups will do their best to help you.

What to Do If You Are Grieving

Here are some ideas that can help you overcome your feelings of grief over a loss. Try as many as you can and see which ones work. Write them down in your journal and write down the results after you try them. This can help you remember which ones work. It can also help you track your progress in overcoming your grief.

- Remember that it takes time to heal. No one gets over grief quickly. The more important someone or something was to you, the longer it can take to get over the loss. Be patient and after a while, the pain won't feel so bad. It's okay if you need some quiet time alone.

- Write a letter to your loved one. Writing a letter can help you get your feelings out. It can also be a way to say good-bye to a person who has died, if you didn't get a chance to do this before. Even though you can't mail it, you can imagine that your loved one is reading it over your shoulder. If you don't feel like writing a letter, draw a picture.

- Forgive yourself. If you're blaming yourself for the person's death, or wish you had said or done something different before your loved one died, it's time to forgive yourself. For example, if you had an argument right before the person died, remember that everyone argues sometimes. It doesn't mean you didn't love each other.

■ Spend time with other people you care about. While this won't replace your loved one, it will remind you that you need to have fun with other people instead of always thinking about the person who died or left.

■ Talk about your loved one whenever you feel you need to. Maybe you feel sad and even cry when you talk about him or her. This is perfectly normal, even though it's hard. But talking helps a lot. Keeping all your feelings inside will make it harder for you to heal.

Lucy's Story

Thirteen-year-old Lucy hasn't been able to shake the blues since Uncle Tommy died. He had been very sick and living with Lucy, her sister, and their mom. After weeks of being sad, Lucy sits down to watch a baseball game on TV, just like she used to with Uncle Tommy. Lucy's mom and sister join her, and soon they are talking about Tommy. He used to have a game on the television every night. They laugh, remembering how happy he'd act when his team won. "It feels good to hear the sounds of a game in the house again," Mom said. "Yeah, it does," Lucy agreed. And just talking about Uncle Tommy felt like a weight was being lifted, even if it was just a little.

■ Talk to your loved one as if he or she can still hear you. This might sound strange, but it really works! Some people believe that people who die go to heaven and can still see and hear what is happening on earth. Thinking about this possibility can help you feel connected with the person who died.

■ Make a scrapbook as a way of remembering your loved one. You can include pictures, letters, things you shared, stories you remember hearing, and facts about the person's life. As you look through the pictures and other things, think about the fun times you shared with the person. You can also draw pictures of you and your loved one—as you remember her or him, or how you wish it could be now. You can even include letters you've written to your loved one after his or her death.

■ Stay busy. This can help you take your mind off of your sadness. You might ride your bike, read, play video games, listen to music, watch movies, build models, work on puzzles, draw, or do other creative things. (See chapter 2 for more tips on making yourself feel better.)

■ Help others. If your loved one died of an illness, you may feel better by helping others who are suffering from the same illness. Some people take part in a walkathon or race to raise money for research to find a cure for the disease. This can be a positive way of coping with your grief.

■ Tell others who are still alive that you care about them. Let them know how much you appreciate them. Thank-you letters and notes are a nice way to do this. You might be surprised how much those cards and letters mean to them, and how much they can help you. Sometimes when people die, we feel bad that we didn't tell them how much we loved them while they were still alive. Telling others that we care for them can be a way of honoring the person who died.

■ Say good-bye to your pet. If it's a pet that has died, have a small funeral and burial for the pet. Saying good-bye this way can help you heal.

■ ■ ■

If these ideas don't seem to help and you're feeling stuck in your grief after many months, ask a family grown-up or other adult you trust for help coping. This person may decide that you would benefit from talking to a counselor. See chapter 10 to learn what it's like to work with a counselor.

Remember: It's normal to feel sad and even mad after you lose someone or something important to you. You may feel that way for a long time. Being patient and trying some of the ideas listed in this chapter can help you get through those feelings a little faster and easier.

Chapter 6

When Sad Feelings Won't Go Away

(Depression)

Most of the time, you can find ways to handle your sad feelings or they go away pretty quickly. When sad feelings stick around, though, they can stop you from doing the things you want or need to do—like eating, going to school, being with friends, or getting exercise. When that happens, you might be depressed.

■ ■ ■

Denny, age ten, feels sad a lot. When he got home from school today he just flopped on the couch to watch TV. His friends called to ask him to join them for inline skating, but he didn't go. He even blew off his homework—he just didn't have the energy. Even though he has lots of friends and does fine in school, he can't help but feel down in the dumps most days. All he wants to do is sleep or watch TV.

■ ■ ■

Keisha, age thirteen, is always grouchy. Most days, it takes very little to set her off. Today she screamed at her friend for tagging her out in softball, her teacher for assigning too much homework, and her mom for asking her to vacuum the living room. She thinks everyone hates her.

■ ■ ■

Being depressed is like trying to drive a boat with the anchor in the water. It holds you back so that you don't have enough energy to move forward—you feel stuck. You might have a few good days when you start feeling better. But then the bad moods come back.

Kinds of Depression

Studies show that at least 6 percent of kids and teens may have depression. This means that in a group of one hundred kids (about three classrooms in school), six of them may be depressed. There are many kinds of depression. Some are more severe than others, and some last longer than others. All forms of depression stop you from feeling good and enjoying life. That's why it's so important to get help—so you can feel good again.

Major Depression

If you've been feeling depressed or irritable almost all of the time for at least two weeks, you may have major depression. This kind of depression can come on quickly. You don't feel like yourself at all and you probably have a very hard time going about your usual activities. You don't feel like doing things you used to think were fun. You also may have some of the following problems almost every day (you have to have at least five to have major depression):

- not feeling like eating OR eating too much

- sleeping too much OR sleeping too little; not being able to fall asleep or stay asleep

- feeling antsy, having too much energy OR moving more slowly

- being tired, not having any energy to do much of anything

- feeling like you're not worth anything

- feeling guilty, even if you didn't do anything wrong

- not being able to concentrate or think clearly

- having trouble making up your mind

- thinking about death or about hurting yourself (see chapter 9 to learn more about suicidal feelings)

Sometimes depression affects boys and girls in different ways. Boys are more likely to feel grouchy or angry, while girls often get quiet and want to be alone.

Dysthymic Disorder

If you've been feeling sad for a year or more, you may have a kind of depression called dysthymic disorder (say it like this: dis-THIGH-mick). This type of depression can develop slowly, so you don't even realize anything is wrong at first. And while it isn't as serious as major depression—you can probably go about your day as normal—it can still cause lots of problems.

Most people with dysthymic disorder usually feel sad most of the day, though not every day. Sometimes kids feel more grouchy or irritable than sad. They may feel better for a while, but this doesn't last more than a couple of weeks or months before they start feeling bad again.

Only a doctor or therapist can tell for sure if you are depressed. That's why it's so important to talk to an adult and get some expert help.

Here are some other signs of dysthymic disorder:

■ not feeling like eating OR eating too much

■ having trouble falling asleep OR sleeping too much

■ not having much energy, feeling tired all the time

■ not feeling good about yourself—having low self-esteem

■ having trouble paying attention or making decisions

■ feeling hopeless—like nothing you do will help

The tricky part of depression, especially with dysthymic disorder, is knowing the difference between being depressed and being temporarily unhappy. That's because a lot of people have these kinds of feelings and problems from time to time. Ask yourself how strong your sad feelings are. Does it feel like the feelings are taking over your life? Are they keeping you from doing well in school or at home? If so, you may be depressed. Only an expert can tell you for sure, though.

SAD—Seasonal Affective Disorder

Does your mood seem to drop during the dark days of winter? If so, you may have a kind of depression called seasonal affective disorder, or SAD. It's called

"seasonal" because it is worse
during certain seasons, usually the
winter. People with SAD often start
feeling sad in November and don't
start feeling better until March or
April. Scientists think SAD is caused
by the lower amount of sunlight during the winter
months. This is why one way to treat SAD is to
spend time under special lamps to replace the
sunlight you don't get during this season.

The symptoms of SAD are the same as those for
major depression. People with SAD may also sleep a
lot, feel hungrier than usual, and gain weight.

Bipolar Disorder

Bipolar disorder is when a person swings from
being depressed to being extremely upset or happy.
When people are in the depressed phase, they have
the same feelings that are described in this chapter.
When they are in the upset or happy phase (known
as the manic phase), they have too many thoughts at
one time, they have problems with having too much
energy, and they have trouble controlling their anger.
See chapter 6 to learn more about bipolar disorder.

Causes of Depression

If you have depression, you probably wonder where
it came from and why it came. You might be embarrassed to be depressed and think it means you're

weak in some way. But depression doesn't have anything to do with being weak or strong—it's an illness that can affect anyone. If you're depressed, what matters is that you get help!

Some people get depressed because of things that happen to them. If a lot of bad things happen, more than you can handle, you might become depressed.

The way your brain works also can affect whether you become depressed. Some people's brains protect them from getting depressed. If your brain chemistry doesn't protect you this way AND bad things happen, you are especially likely to get depressed.

Your brain has a number of parts. Each part communicates with other parts, and all parts need to work together for you to do your best and to feel happy. When certain brain chemicals called *neurotransmitters* are out of balance, you're more likely to become depressed. Medicines can help people with depression balance these brain chemicals.

Depression can also be inherited. If someone in your family has problems with depression, you might, too.

Many famous people have been depressed. Terry Bradshaw is a Hall of Fame quarterback who was called Pittsburgh's "Man of Steel." He led four Pittsburgh Steelers teams to Super Bowl titles and won the National Football League's Most Valuable Player award in 1978. Yet after games, he would break down into tears. He became even more depressed after he retired from football. Finally, with the help of counseling and medicine, he was able to beat his depression.

Some medical problems also can cause depression. For instance, your thyroid gland, which makes growth hormones, also helps control your moods. If it's not working right, you may get depressed. Diabetes is another illness that can cause depression. A healthcare professional can do tests to find out if you have any physical problem that could be causing depression.

Some medicines people take for other health problems can have a side effect of depression. If you're on any medications and you start feeling sad a lot, ask your mom or dad to schedule a checkup for you.

Scientists are working hard to figure out all the causes of depression so they can find better ways to treat it. Even though you can't control whether you get depression, you can decide what to do about it.

What to Do If You Have Depression

You need the help of an expert to know whether you're dealing with depression. If a doctor or therapist says you have depression, what might happen next?

You'll probably begin meeting with a counselor to talk about your feelings. Your

Even if your feelings don't match all of the symptoms of depression described in this chapter, if you're feeling down, please still get help. Sad feelings can get worse with time, so don't ignore your sad feelings. Do something about them. Begin by talking to a caring adult.

counselor can help you with the exercises in this
book and suggest other ways you can help yourself.
Read chapter 10 to learn more about what it's like to
work with a counselor.

A counselor can also help figure out what kind
of depression you have and whether you might
need medicine. Medicines that help people with
depression are called *antidepressants*. They change
how your brain chemicals work, often by making
them work harder. For some kids, the depression can
only get better with antidepressants. If your doctor
prescribes a medication for you, be sure to follow
the directions. It won't help if you refuse or forget
to take it.

Besides meeting with a counselor and maybe taking medicine, you can do lots of things on your own to help you deal with your feelings of depression. Try the ideas in this chapter to see which ones work for you. It might take a while before they start working. But don't give up—keep at it!

Create a Mood Chart

Using a calendar or your journal, rate how you feel each day. You can find out if there is a pattern to your moods. Maybe you feel worse during the week, which might be a clue that school is adding to your problems. Or you might discover that you feel better on the days when you exercise. This tells you that exercise helps!

Warning: Although it doesn't happen often, medicines that usually help kids with depression can sometimes make them feel worse. They might feel more edgy, too sleepy, or more depressed. If any of these things happen to you, tell your mom or dad right away! Your parent can call the doctor to figure out what to do.

Also, don't stop taking a medicine for depression without talking to your doctor first. Since these medicines change how your brain chemicals work, stopping suddenly can be dangerous. Even if you don't think the medicine is helping, stopping on your own can cause your depression to return—sometimes after just a few days.

The first thing is to rate your feelings on a scale from 0 to 10, with 0 meaning you feel good and you're happy, 10 meaning you feel as depressed as you can imagine, and 5 meaning you feel somewhere in the middle.

Sometimes, it's more helpful to rate yourself two or three times a day. You can give yourself a number for the mornings, afternoons, and evenings. Maybe you feel bad in the mornings, but feel better as the day goes on. This is common in people who are depressed.

You can make your chart more interesting by using colors if you want. For example, use black to mean you're very sad that day, blue to mean you're moderately sad, and yellow to mean your day is a good one, filled with sunshine.

If you're taking medicine for depression, keeping a mood chart can also help your doctor figure out if it's working. After you've been keeping a chart for a while, bring it with you to your next checkup. Maybe you need a higher dose or a different medicine. Maybe you need to take your medicine at a different time of the day. Be sure to let your doctor make those decisions. NEVER decide on your own to change how much medicine you take.

Untwist Your Thinking

Many people who are depressed think about things in ways that aren't really true, which makes them feel worse. By catching yourself when you think this way, you can help yourself feel better. Look through your journal for twisted thinking, then practice untwisting those thoughts. Here are some examples:

- If one bad thing happens, everything else will turn out bad. Of course this isn't true. Just because you fail one test doesn't mean you'll fail every test for the rest of your life! It's just one test.

- Good things that happen don't count; bad things that happen count a lot. If something good happens to you, do you think it's just an accident and that good things won't keep happening? Or maybe you don't even notice when good things happen because you're so busy looking for bad things. For instance, if you have this kind of twisted thinking and someone tells you that you look nice, you might think the person is lying. Then if someone makes fun of you, you might make a big deal about it and let it ruin your whole day. A better way to handle it is to make a big deal of anything *good* that happens.

■   Everyone has to like me, otherwise I'm worthless. Not everyone will like you, just like you probably don't like everyone you meet. It's okay if people don't like you. Maybe you just don't like the same things.

■   I have to be perfect. If I make a mistake, it means I'm a failure. No one is perfect! Everyone makes mistakes. It's important to learn to laugh at your mistakes and tell yourself it's not a disaster to goof up. Remember, all famous inventors in the world made lots of mistakes before they got it right. Imagine if the Wright brothers, the inventors of the airplane, gave up after their first plane crashed. They learned from each mistake. Mistakes teach us what we did wrong, so we can do it better next time.

■ ■ ■

Fighting depression takes time and work, but you can do it. Use the ideas in this chapter and work with your grown-up helper to find experts who can help you get started. You can find ways to overcome your sad feelings and feel better again.

Chapter 7

Roller-Coaster Moods

(Bipolar Disorder)

Farouk, age eleven, has mood swings. Last week he was in a super good mood. He felt like he could do anything. He'd get the giggles and couldn't stop. But this week he's been waking up feeling grouchy. This morning he yelled at his mom when she tried to hurry him up for school, then started screaming because his cereal was too soggy. He had a tantrum at school because he couldn't stay focused on his work. Sometimes he thinks his family would be better off without him.

■ ■ ■

Most people have days when they feel down or low and days when things feel pretty good. You can think of these normal mood changes as the bumps at the beginning or end of most roller-coaster rides—they're over pretty quickly and they're not too big. But Farouk has bipolar disorder. Bipolar disorder is more like the highest and lowest points of a roller coaster. There are climbs to the tops of towering hills and then stomach-tumbling rides to valleys far below. For Farouk and other people with bipolar disorder, though, the ride isn't fun at all—it feels out of control and they don't know when it will end.

The word *bipolar* means "two poles"—a low one and a high one. The low part is depression and the high part is *mania*. Mania is when a person feels extremely happy, fidgety, or energetic—or all three. When people experience mania, they are *manic*. People who have bipolar disorder bounce from being depressed to being manic very quickly. Some kids have both phases at the same time. That's called a mixed state.

Sometimes, kids who are younger than 12, can have disruptive mood dysregulation disorder instead. Kids with this disorder don't switch between mania and depression like someone with bipolar disorder. These kids have severe tantrums and are irritable and angry a lot of the time. Most of the ideas in this chapter can help you with either disorder.

Doctors aren't sure how many kids have bipolar disorder. Experts estimate 1 to 5 percent. This means somewhere between one and five out of every 100 kids may have bipolar disorder.

What It's Like to Have Bipolar Disorder

Bipolar disorder affects how people think, feel, and behave; how their body feels; and whether they can do the things they want and need to do. Having bipolar disorder is different from regular mood changes. With this illness, people's moods are extreme and their reactions to what's going on are extreme, too—or their reactions might even have nothing to do with what's happening in their life.

While only a doctor or counselor can say for sure if you have bipolar disorder, kids with this illness usually have some symptoms of both depression and mania. You can learn about depression and its symptoms in chapter 6. Here are some symptoms of mania. Kids who are manic may:

- feel like they're better than others or that they can do anything they want

- not need much sleep and not feel tired

- talk a lot, or feel like they can't stop talking

- have one thought after another, or feel like their thoughts are racing

- have trouble paying attention, or get distracted by unimportant things

- feel like they have to accomplish a goal no matter what, or feel too wound up

- get involved in things that can get them into big trouble, like fighting, stealing, taking dangerous risks (like on a bike or skateboard), or taking drugs or drinking alcohol

Bipolar disorder can look different, depending on how many symptoms a person has. The more symptoms people experience, the more difficult it is to go about their day as normal—they have problems doing well in school, getting along with their family at home, and keeping friendships going.

Another way bipolar disorder affects different people in different ways is with the number of mood changes they have. Some kids have mood changes only a few times a year, but others bounce back and forth between these extreme moods every week or even in a single day. Kids are more likely to have quick changes in their mood, while adults can feel sad for weeks or months and then switch to feeling too good for weeks or months.

Other Symptoms of Bipolar Disorder

Kids with bipolar disorder often have other problems. They may:

- overreact to little problems

- have trouble being flexible and not getting their way

- have tantrums that can last hours

- have night terrors—bad nightmares in which they wake up screaming

- have overly silly or goofy moods

- be afraid to be away from their mom, dad, or other caregiver

- be afraid of dying or death

- have trouble switching from one activity to the next

One of the hardest parts of bipolar disorder is having rages (or meltdowns). Rages can come on suddenly, without any warning. Maybe this has happened to you. One minute you're feeling fine, the next minute you're out of control—screaming, throwing things, having violent thoughts, and saying mean things you usually wouldn't say. You might break things that belong to you or others. You might even threaten to hurt others. Often, rages are triggered by being told you can't do something, but sometimes they happen for no reason. It's as if the thinking part of the brain shuts down. Meltdowns can last minutes or hours.

Some kids say a rage feels like a monster has taken over their body. Others say it's like a storm that rolls in. Like storms, sometimes rages build up over the course of a day and sometimes they seem to come out of nowhere. After the storm dumps its rain, things calm down quickly. Some kids feel very tired and even fall asleep after a rage. They might also feel bad about it afterward, though some kids don't even remember what happened.

If you have bipolar disorder, it's not your fault that you have rages. You still have to take responsibility for them, though. If you can't avoid a meltdown or it hits you without warning, be sure to apologize when it's over for anything you said or did that was hurtful.

If you have rages, it can be terribly scary—for you and those around you. You might feel "crazy" and frustrated that you can't control your feelings or behavior. You don't know when you will go off next. The best thing you can do to help yourself is talk to a family adult or your counselor about the problem you're having. They may be able to help you figure out the signs that you're going into a rage. Some kids feel hot before it starts. Others feel funny or grouchy. Once you know the signs, you might be able to do something to avoid a meltdown. A doctor can also determine whether you should take medicine to treat bipolar disorder, and this can help a lot with rages.

Another common part of bipolar disorder is that you might get an idea in your mind that becomes "stuck." Two experts on bipolar disorder—Dr. Demitri Papolos and Janice Papolos—have named this "mission mode." If you experience this, you might feel like you're on a mission to do something and get very mad if anyone tries to take you away from it. You can't get the thought out of your mind, so you might keep asking for something, even if your parents have said no many times. This causes arguments, which can lead to rages. Or, you might insist on doing something a certain way, even if it isn't working.

What Causes Bipolar Disorder?

Scientists are still studying the causes of bipolar disorder. We do know that, like other kinds of depression, it runs in families. If you have a parent or other relative with bipolar disorder, chances are greater that you might have it, too. Or, if you have a relative who has problems with depression or abuses drugs or alcohol, your chances are also higher. This doesn't mean you're *likely* to have it, though.

The way the brain works may also cause bipolar disorder. The part of the brain in charge of emotions, called the *limbic system*, may be overly active in people with bipolar disorder. When they have a meltdown, it's like this part of their brain "hijacks" the rest of it. The limbic system overreacts and shuts off the part of their brain that makes decisions and solves problems, called the *prefrontal cortex*. So their emotions end up bubbling over, but their thinking is shut down so they can't think about how to handle their frustrations.

How Can You Treat Bipolar Disorder?

If an expert tells you that you have bipolar disorder, that person will probably help develop a treatment plan for you, or will refer you to another expert who will do this. Although treatment won't make bipolar disorder go away, it will help you keep it under control so you can stay more balanced and help yourself be successful and happy.

Medicine

Part of your treatment might include taking medicines called mood stabilizers. Medicines used to treat bipolar disorder help the brain stay calm and not overreact to things as much. Often, kids need more than one medicine to treat the different symptoms of bipolar disorder. One might help control the big changes, another might help with depression, and a third might help prevent meltdowns. Adults with bipolar disorder usually have to stay on medicine for years, but doctors and scientists are not sure if this is true for children. Ask your doctor about this and any other questions you have about taking medications.

If you're taking medicine for bipolar disorder, be sure to take it every day. Your mom or dad can probably help with this. Forgetting or refusing to take the pills can cause more problems.

While medicines can help a lot, they sometimes have side effects—unwanted symptoms caused by the medicine. Some of the more common side effects of medicines for bipolar disorder include sleepiness, increased hunger, upset stomach, and extreme thirst. Usually these effects go away after a few weeks. If they don't or if you start to feel worse, be sure to tell your doctor. Your doctor may be able to make changes in how much you take or switch to a new medicine.

Warning: If you start having thoughts about hurting yourself or others, be sure to have your parents contact the doctor right away. Sometimes, medicines can trigger these thoughts in children.

Counseling

Another important part of treatment for bipolar disorder is counseling, or therapy. Counseling is important because you can learn more about bipolar disorder and ways to handle it. For example, a counselor can help you learn how to cope with your anger and sadness, and how to explain your rages to friends who might otherwise be scared off by them. With a counselor, you may practice apologizing if you overreact and say or do unkind things to family members or friends. For more information on counseling, read chapter 10.

Things You Can Do to Help Yourself

In addition to getting therapy and taking medication, there are other ways you can help yourself deal with bipolar disorder. Here are some ideas you can try.

Rate Your Moods

Rating your moods is a good way to let your family grown-ups or teachers know how bad you're feeling. That way, they'll know whether you need some help.

You can use the following scale:

1 = I'm feeling fine, no problems with anger or sadness.

2 = I'm feeling a bit angry or sad, but I can ignore it or keep myself busy.

3 = I'm feeling angry or sad, but with help I think I'll be able to calm down. I'll try doing something different to take my mind off my feelings.

4 = I'm feeling more angry or sad, and I'm starting to feel out of control. With help, I may be able to calm down but I'm not sure.

5 = I'm feeling very angry or sad. I'm over-whelmed and out of control.

Talk to your family adults or teachers about how you'll show them your mood rating. For example, you could hang a dry-erase board on your bed post or bedroom door. Then each morning, you could write your mood number on the board for your family to see. In school you could give your teacher a piece of paper with your rating each morning.

If it's easier for you, you can also use a color code such as the one that many schools use.

Green day = feeling fine

Yellow day = having some problems with anger and sadness, but I haven't lost control yet

Red day = feeling very angry or sad, and I'm not able to control it

Recognize Triggers

Often, certain feelings or events can set off a mood change or a rage. If you can learn to recognize these triggers, you may be able to prevent them. For example, if being late in the morning is one of your triggers, you can start going to bed earlier and getting up earlier.

Make a list of your triggers. You can do this in your journal if you want. Ask your family grown-up to help you make the list. A good time to do this is right after you've felt manic, when it's still fresh in your mind. Check your list every week to make sure you're not missing anything.

Franco's Story

Franco, age ten, had a lot of rages at home and at school—he would lose control and end up yelling and throwing things around. The worst part was he couldn't figure out what was making him melt down. Franco decided to ask his teacher and dad if they saw any clues to his behavior.

They helped him see that he had two main triggers. One was feeling overloaded by schoolwork. The other was when he had to stop playing video games at night to do his homework.

Franco worked out a signal with his teacher. When he started feeling upset in class, he would pull on his ear. His teacher would notice and ask him to take some papers to the office. This gave Franco a chance to calm down before he lost his cool. At home, he and his dad agreed that he would do his homework before playing video games. Then he would avoid the trigger of having to stop playing to finish homework. These changes were hard to get used to at first, but he could tell the difference right away. He had fewer rages, and it felt good to have some control over his moods.

Handle Angry Feelings and Extra Energy

A big part of learning to deal with bipolar disorder is finding ways to handle angry feelings that come up. Some kids feel better if they can hit a punching bag or pillow when they're feeling very angry. This is a lot better than hitting your brother, sister, mom, or dad.

CAUTION: Some kids feel MORE angry and upset when they hit something. If this happens to you, don't use a punching bag or pillow. Try counting to ten or something else to relax you.

Getting enough exercise is another good way to release angry feelings. When you get into a bad mood, often you get an extra burst of energy. By going running, doing jumping jacks, jumping rope, or doing other activities, you can use up that extra energy and help calm yourself.

You can also use extra energy to be helpful. Get ahead on your homework. If you can't concentrate on your homework (which is often true when your mood changes), volunteer to clean up at home. Clean the closet, your drawers, or under the bed. These are all ways of using up that extra energy. But don't overdo it. Try to get enough sleep if you can. Following a schedule of going to bed at the same time each night and getting up at the same time each morning also can help a lot with bipolar disorder.

People with bipolar disorder can be very creative when it comes to things like drawing, painting, sculpting, writing stories or songs, and other arts. When you have extra energy and a lot of ideas, try painting or writing down your ideas. You might be surprised what you come up with!

Sometimes, eating something when you're feeling depressed or on the edge can help put you in a better mood. If you notice that your mood is starting to change and it's been a while since you last ate, ask for something to eat. Avoid sugar or junk food, though.

Control Stress

If you can feel your moods changing, try to keep your stress under control. Listen to some music, go for a quiet walk, or put on a relaxation tape. Take a warm bath or read a book. Stay close to home and don't take on new projects that might be too frustrating. This is not the time to build a model airplane!

Most of the ideas listed in chapters 2, 3, and 6 also can help with bipolar disorder. Be sure to read each idea carefully and see which ones work for you the best. And don't give up if they don't work at first. You have to practice!

■ ■ ■

Living with bipolar disorder can be challenging. You'll need to work at recognizing when your moods are changing and try different ways to keep them under control. You'll probably need to work with a counselor and take medications to help, too. The good news is that lots of people want to help you—you don't have to do it alone. Together with your helpers, you can find ways to live a calmer, happier life.

Chapter 8

Other Problems Related to Depression

Sometimes being sad or depressed for a long time can lead to other big problems. Or, just as often, other big problems can cause a person to feel sad or depressed. If one of these problems is affecting you, you might find it hard to get over feeling down no matter what you do. You may need to deal with the other problem first. And to do that, you may need to find help.

This chapter talks about these kinds of problems—bullying, eating disorders, drug and alcohol use, and abuse and neglect—and it gives you lots of ideas on how to find the help you need if one of them is affecting you. Maybe you have the problem, or maybe a person you're close to is having the problem. Whether it's you or someone you love, it can make you feel very cranky and blue. It's important to remember that help is out there. You are not alone!

Bullying

Have you ever had other students push you around at school, tease you or call you names, take your stuff, threaten to hurt you if you didn't do what they said, or spread rumors about you that aren't true? These can be forms of bullying. While this can happen to anyone once in a while, if it's happening to you a lot, you probably feel sad, upset, and even angry about it. It might get to the point where you don't even want to go to school. Maybe you're scared to tell anyone. But if you're being bullied, you need to speak up and tell someone. No one deserves to be treated this way. You don't need to handle it all by yourself.

> If you're the one doing the bullying—which some kids do if they're sad, lonely, or angry a lot—you can change. Start by apologizing to people you've bullied. Try to be a friend to those people by inviting them to play with you and sticking up for them when someone bullies them. Doing these things can make you feel a lot better. If you need help, ask an adult at home or at school.

What to Do If You're Being Bullied

If you're being bullied, tell your teacher, your parents, or your principal. Let them know that you're upset by the behavior and that you want it to stop. If school officials know it's happening, they can work to stop the bullying.

There are ways to make it harder for kids to pick on you. On the bus, sit in front near the driver. Kids who want to bully aren't as likely to try anything if they know an adult is nearby. Try to stick with friends when walking down the halls or outside. Don't go into restrooms alone.

Eating Disorders

Sometimes, people who are depressed develop eating disorders—unhealthy patterns of eating that can lead to serious medical problems or even death. Many people eat more to make themselves feel better, others lose their appetite and eat less. While the amount of food most people eat varies a little each day, with an eating disorder, the change in eating is more severe. Even so, the people around someone with a disorder might not notice how much or how little that person is eating. That's because a common part of eating disorders is trying to hide it. For example, people with eating disorders might get up in the middle of the night to sneak food, stash food in their room, or pretend they have to go to the bathroom after dinner so they can throw up.

There are different kinds of eating disorders. Anorexia is probably the best known. People who are anorexic think they are too fat no matter how thin they are. They might be the thinnest person in their class but see themselves as fat. This is part of the disorder. They try to eat as little as possible. Bulimia is another type of eating disorder. People with bulimia go on eating binges—they eat an extreme amount of food in a very short time. If they eat this much food, they might feel sick afterward and guilty about how much they ate. They may make themselves throw up or take pills called laxatives that make them go to the bathroom a lot. Or they might exercise a lot—sometimes for hours a day.

Eating disorders do more than affect a person's weight. They can damage the body in ways that last a lifetime. Not eating enough can injure or weaken organs and bones. Making yourself throw up can damage the esophagus, cause tooth decay, and create stomach ulcers. It can lead to low levels of minerals, which can make you tired or even cause heart problems. Eating disorders are more common in girls than boys, but the percentage of boys who have them is growing.

What to Do If You Have an Eating Disorder

If you have some of these symptoms, it's very important that you get professional help. Even if it's scary to ask for help, please talk to a family grown-up as soon as possible. At your age, it's more important than ever to take good care of your body by eating a healthy, balanced diet.

If a doctor or counselor tells you that you have an eating disorder, she or he will help you develop a plan so you can get better. Sometimes this plan involves going to the hospital for a while. A number of different professionals may be part of your treatment team—including a trained counselor, a doctor, and a dietician.

If you have both an eating disorder and depression, getting help for your depression may also help you overcome your eating disorder. If you start feeling better about yourself in general, your problems with food may go away. But if your eating disorder is severe, you might have to work on the eating disorder before you can treat your depression.

You can contact the National Association of Anorexia Nervosa and Associated Disorders to get free helpline counseling (Monday through Friday, 9 a.m. to 5 p.m. Central time), to find groups who can give you support, and to get contact information for healthcare professionals who can help you. You can also learn more about eating disorders and how to prevent them. Contact them at (630) 577-1330 or www.anad.org.

Drug or Alcohol Use

When people are sad or depressed, some turn to alcohol or other drugs to help them forget about their problems. Some kids drink beer or wine; smoke marijuana or cigarettes; or even sniff, or "huff," chemicals around the house to feel better or get high. Others take medicines that are prescribed for someone else.

While alcohol and other drugs can seem to help at first, they cause far more problems than they solve. Because kids are still growing, they can become addicted to drugs or alcohol faster than adults. Drugs and alcohol can kill someone who takes too much. They can stop the person's heart or breathing. They can cause cancer or harm organs, such as the liver, heart, or kidneys. And if you are taking medicine, using drugs or alcohol can be even more dangerous. For these reasons, you should never turn to drugs or alcohol to feel better. Tell a grown-up right away if you are tempted to try them.

Maybe it's not you who has a problem with drugs or alcohol. Millions of children have family members who use drugs or drink too much alcohol. Some adults can drink alcohol and not have any problems (you have to be 21 to legally drink in the United States). But others drink too much or too often. When people drink a lot or use other drugs, their behavior changes, making them act silly, angry, or unpredictable. Their drinking or drug use can cause problems with their families, their jobs, and can even lead to trouble with the law. If drug or alcohol abuse is happening in your home, you may be worried about your safety or the safety of people you love. You may have more chores to do if others aren't doing their share. Or you may be too embarrassed to bring friends home because your parent might be drunk or high. Things like that can make you feel sad or lonely.

The main thing to remember is that it's not your fault when a parent or other family member drinks too much or uses drugs—even if this person tries to blame it on you.

What to Do If Drug or Alcohol Use Is a Problem for You or Someone in Your Family

If you've been using alcohol or other drugs, it's very important that you stop. Let a family adult know what you've been going through. If you try to stop and find you keep using alcohol or drugs again, you may need a counselor to help you find ways to quit. (See chapter 10 for more on working with a counselor.)

It can be hard to share this problem with family adults because you're probably afraid they'll be mad. They may be upset at first, but if you tell them that you realize it's a problem and that you need their help, chances are they'll be more understanding. If they are angry or won't listen, you can still get help from an adult at school or in your faith community.

If your family adult is the one with the drug or alcohol problem, talk to another adult about it. You can also contact the National Association for Children of Alcoholics for help. Their website has a section just for kids: www.nacoa.org/kidspage.htm.

Abuse and Neglect

Sometimes adults or older children will abuse, or hurt, younger kids. The hurt can be physical, meaning that the kid's body is harmed. Abuse can also be verbal or emotional—saying mean or cruel things to someone or acting in a mean or cruel way. Some abuse is sexual— meaning it involves a person's private parts. A few examples of abuse include pinching, kicking, or hitting with belts or sticks; burning people; swearing at people, calling them names, or telling them they're no good.

While parents in the United States and Canada are allowed to spank their kids if they misbehave, sometimes spanking turns into abuse, especially if it leaves bruises or marks on the body.

Abuse can also happen with other members of your family, such as between your mom and dad. Knowing that one of your parents is being hurt can be hard to deal with, especially since you may feel helpless to do anything. Talk to your teacher or school counselor if abuse is happening in your home.

Neglect is another problem that can happen to kids. This occurs when their parents or caregivers don't take care of them the way they're supposed to. Neglect could include:

■ not taking kids to the doctor when they're sick

■ not feeding kids enough or providing them with clothes to wear

- not watching kids carefully, resulting in them getting hurt

- leaving kids alone at home before they're old enough to take care of themselves

- allowing kids to use alcohol or other drugs

- not requiring kids to attend school

- not taking kids to a counselor if they have emotional problems

What to Do If You're Being Abused or Neglected

It is against the law for parents or other caregivers to abuse or neglect you. If any of these things have happened to you or are happening to you or someone you know, tell a family grown-up, counselor, teacher, principal, or other adult you trust. Talk to someone even if you're not sure that what is happening is really abuse. If it doesn't feel right to you, talk to an adult about it. That person can help you figure out what to do.

If you need immediate help or have been injured, call 911. If someone has been hurting you or you have questions about child abuse, call Childhelp USA's National Child Abuse Hotline at 1-800-4-A-CHILD (1-800-422-4453). They have counselors who can help you figure out what to do. The hotline is always open. It's totally private—the counselor doesn't know who you are and won't ask for your name. (Check out their website for online help or if you don't need to talk to someone but want more information about abuse: www.childhelp.org/pages/help-for-kids1.)

You can also report abuse by calling a local abuse hotline listed in the Yellow Pages or by calling the local police at 911.

When you call the police or a local abuse hotline for help, the person you talk to will ask you what happened, who abused you, and where that person lives. He or she will also ask your name and age, where you live, and what school you go to. A day or two after your call, someone from that agency may come to your home or school to talk with you about what happened and figure out what to do so you'll be safe.

Telling may be difficult, especially if the person who is hurting you is a loved one. But this person needs help and telling can help make that happen.

■ ■ ■

This chapter talked about some of the big problems that can lead kids to feeling sad or depressed. But lots of other things can lead to these feelings, too. If you have a problem that makes it harder for you to do well in school, get along with others, or feel good about yourself, it's important to get help for that problem and to understand it. That will help you figure out how to handle it the best way you can. Remember, you can ask for what you need and people will help you!

Chapter 9

When You Feel Like Giving Up on Life
(Suicide)

Some kids feel so depressed they get tired of living. They can't handle the pain of being depressed or they think a problem is just too big to handle, and they lose hope that things will ever get better. When this happens, they might start thinking about hurting themselves or dying. Taking your own life is called *suicide*. Thoughts about suicide are called *suicidal thoughts*. In this chapter, you'll learn about this very serious problem and what you can do if you ever feel suicidal.

Actually, most kids who think about suicide don't really want to die. They just want to stop the sadness and anger they feel, and they don't think anything else will work. But this isn't true! There are many ways to treat depression. If one thing doesn't work, you can try another. You *can* feel better!

■ ■ ■

Melanie, age eleven, feels sad almost all the time. Her father left her family and she hasn't seen him in a year. She thinks no one loves her and feels bad that her mom has to work full-time and take care of

Melanie and her sisters. Melanie doesn't see any way out of her problems, so she starts thinking about death. If she were dead, her mother wouldn't have to worry about her anymore. She knows this doesn't make a lot of sense, but she thinks about it anyway. Lately, her thoughts are scaring her.

■ ■ ■

Alfonso, age twelve, feels sad and angry. He's mad at all the kids who have made fun of him at school. He's upset that his dad called him a loser because he got an F on his report card. For a while he thinks the only way to stop feeling so lousy is to stop living. But then he talks to his school counselor, and she helps him see that to feel better he has to stay alive. She connects him with a doctor who can help him get over his depression and feel good again.

What to Do If You're Thinking About Suicide

If you feel like hurting yourself in *any* way, TELL A GROWN-UP RIGHT AWAY! These are serious thoughts and if you have them, it means you need help NOW. If it feels hard to bring it up, here are some things you can say to start talking:

■ "Sometimes, I feel like life isn't worth living anymore. Can you help me not feel this way?"

- "I'm having thoughts about dying and I don't know what to do. I need your help."

- "I have something really important I need to talk about. I feel like hurting myself—can you help me?"

 If no one is at home and you can't reach another grown-up, call 911. Or, call a crisis hotline and talk to an emergency counselor. You can call the numbers listed below at any time—seven days a week, twenty-four hours a day—and someone will help you. You can also go to their websites to learn more about coping with tough problems. Copy these numbers in your journal or on an index card and carry them with you:

Covenant House Nineline
1-800-999-9999
www.nineline.org

SAFE Alternatives
1-800-366-8288
www.selfinjury.com

National Hopeline Network
1-800-784-2433
www.hopeline.com

The Trevor Project
(for lesbian, gay, bisexual, transgender, and questioning youth)
1-866-488-7386
www.thetrevorproject.org

When you call to ask for help, you'll be asked questions about your suicidal thoughts. Be honest so the person can help you.

What's important is that you let someone else know about the pain you're dealing with and ask for help. Don't give up until you find someone who will listen to you and is able to help.

If you're doing okay right now but have had thoughts about hurting yourself before, one important thing you can do is to make a list of people you can call when you're feeling suicidal. Ask them if it's okay to put them on your list and what times of the day you can call them. Get their home number, their work number, and their cell phone number, if they have one. Talking about your feelings can make it easier to deal with them. Ask the people on your list to remind you of all the reasons life is worth living. Keep the list in your journal or copy it onto an index card and carry it with you.

Make a Promise

If you're having thoughts of wanting to die, your counselor (or an emergency counselor, if you don't have your own counselor) may ask you to promise not to do anything to harm yourself until she or he can talk to you again. You can also make that promise to your family grown-ups. Making a promise helps keep you safe until you can get more help. It also gives the suicidal thoughts a chance to fade away. Some counselors may ask you to sign a contract promising not to hurt yourself.

You can make a promise to yourself, too. Tell yourself that at least for today, you won't hurt yourself. Just think about getting through today. This gives counseling and medicine more time to start working. Remember, treatment takes time to work. Some medicines that help with feeling depressed and suicidal can take a few weeks to start working. Try to be patient. If your medicine is taking more than a few weeks to help, you may need a bigger dose. Or you may need to try a different medicine. There *is* a way you can feel better. Don't lose hope if it doesn't happen right away.

If you're taking medicine for depression and you have suicidal thoughts, have a family adult call your doctor RIGHT AWAY. If your suicidal thoughts started soon after you began taking the medicine or if your doctor just increased your dosage, your thoughts may be caused by the medicine. Your doctor may need to change how much you take or switch you to a different medicine. But don't stop taking the medicine on your own.

■ ■ ■

Having thoughts about suicide is scary for you and your family. These thoughts are sometimes part of feeling depressed. With help, you can learn how to beat those thoughts and stay safe until you start feeling better.

Chapter 10

How Experts Can Help

Practicing the ideas in this book can help you a lot if you're cranky, blue, or depressed, but it's possible you'll need counseling or therapy, too. A counselor or therapist is a person you can talk to about your problems. Below are some of the most frequently asked questions about counseling, as well as answers that may help.

#1: What happens in counseling?

The counselor will listen to your problems and give you ideas about how to handle them. Your counselor will ask you questions to learn about your feelings. Together, you can come up with ideas that will help you. Then you can practice the ideas at home. The counselor is also there to answer any questions you have about feeling sad or lonely, or other problems in your life.

It may take time for counseling to work. A lot depends on how well you get along with your counselor and whether you try the ideas he or she suggests. Give this person a chance, but if the sessions don't seem to be working for you, talk to a family adult. You may need to try different counselors until you meet one you really like.

#2: Who will be there?

Most of the time, an adult from your family will come to your first session to sign papers and talk about what you've been going through. After that, you can go to the sessions alone, or you can bring along a family adult if you want to. Having a family grown-up there may help you feel more comfortable, and that person can learn ways to help you at home. Sometimes, older brothers or sisters might be included in a session, if you'd like that to happen.

#3: Why do I have to talk about my problems?

No one will make you talk if you don't want to. Some kids feel embarrassed about telling their problems to a stranger. Others don't want to admit to having problems. This is normal. It may take a while to get to know your counselor, and you may not say much at first. After you feel comfortable, it will be easier to talk. Remember that talking about your problems is much more helpful than keeping them bottled up inside.

The counselor can't help you if you keep your problems a secret. If you're scared or angry about meeting with the counselor, start out by telling the counselor your feelings. If your counselor suggests an idea that you don't like, tell the counselor how you feel about it and ask for a different idea.

#4: Won't everyone find out about my problem?

Your visits with your counselor are *confidential*, which means that your counselor isn't allowed to tell anyone else about your problems. The only time a counselor has to tell your parents about what you say is if you tell the counselor that you're thinking about hurting or killing yourself or someone else, or if someone is hurting you. This is to protect you.

You can decide if you want to tell other people in your family what you're learning in counseling. And it's up to you whether you tell your friends about what's going on. If you have friends you trust, it may help you to talk to them about your sad feelings.

#5: Does my mom or dad have to talk to the counselor, too?

If your parents brought you to a counselor, this probably means they're not sure how to help you with your problems. Your counselor can explain the problem to your parents so they can understand you better and give you the help you need. Counseling often works best if parents are involved, too. (They don't have to talk to the counselor at the same time you do.) Parents need to know what to do when kids feel sad or have mood swings. If you want your counselor to keep some of the things you say private, be sure to let him or her know that.

#6: Does my teacher have to know about this?

If your sadness isn't affecting your schoolwork, no one at school needs to know that you're in counseling. If your sadness involves problems with school, your counselor may want to talk with your teacher to give suggestions on how to help you. If you have bipolar disorder, it will help for your teacher to understand why you get so upset sometimes, even when everything seems to be going well. By law, your counselor can't talk with anyone at your school unless your parents give permission. If you don't want this to happen, let your counselor and your parents know.

#7: How long do I have to go to the counselor?

Some kids may need to go just a few times, but others may need to go every week for a few months or longer. It depends on what the problem is, how hard you work at it, and how quickly you improve. Be patient, because it can take a while for counseling to help.

Sometimes, counseling isn't enough and you may need medication as well. If you think counseling isn't helping, for whatever reason, talk to your parents and your counselor about it.

#8: What about medication?

If you get so sad and depressed that you can't get rid of those feelings no matter how hard you try, you may need medication to help you. If this happens, a doctor will ask you questions about your sad feelings and figure out which medication will work best in your situation. Most kids with bipolar disorder will need to be on medicine to help control their mood swings.

A lot of times, when you have problems with depression or bipolar disorder, it's because the chemicals in your brain aren't working the right way. Medicines help these chemicals work harder, or work the right way, so that feelings of sadness start to fade.

Doctors have many different medications they can use to help. Each one works in a different way, and the doctor may not know which one will work best until you try it. You may have to try more than one medication, or even take two different ones at the same time, before you find something that works.

Some medications can cause side effects, such as headaches, stomachaches, or sleepiness. They can make your mouth dry, make you yawn a lot, or cause you to gain weight. Sometimes, a medication may actually make your problems worse, such as making it harder to fall asleep. Because people react in different ways to different medications, there's no way to tell how a medication may affect you. If you have side effects you don't like, talk to your parents and counselor. The side effects may go away after a few weeks as your body gets used to the medication. If they don't, you might have to try a different one until your doctor finds one that's right for you. **WARNING:** If you start having thoughts about hurting yourself or others, be sure to have your parents contact the doctor right away. Sometimes, medicines can trigger these thoughts in children.

It's important to take the medication the way your doctor tells you, which usually means every day. Don't stop taking it on your own or take more of it, since this can cause problems. If you have questions about the medication or want to take more or less, *always* talk to your parents and your doctor first.

#9: What if we can't afford counseling?

It is possible to find free or low-cost counseling services, depending on your family's needs. You can start by talking to your school counselor or your principal about special services that may be available through your school district. Your mom or dad can look in the Yellow Pages for low-cost counseling services, or contact a county social worker for more information. Most medical insurance plans will help pay the cost of some counseling sessions.

#10: What more can I do?

On page 113, you'll find a "Note to Grown-Ups" that you can share with your family adult. It will give him or her ideas for helping you handle your problems and on working together to manage your sad and blue feelings. On pages 118–120, you'll find a list of other resources that may be of help, too.

Resources

Hot Stuff to Help Kids Cheer Up: The Depression and Self-Esteem Workbook by Jerry Wilde (Naperville, IL: Sourcebooks Jaberwocky, 2007). Good help for working through depression and self-esteem issues.

"I Wish I Could Hold Your Hand—": A Child's Guide to Grief and Loss by Pat Palmer (San Luis Obispo, CA: Impact Publishers, 1994). Learn more about grieving feelings.

My Listening Friend by P.J. Michaels (Plainsview, NY: Childswork/Childsplay, 2001). A child's story of going to a counselor for the first time.

What to Do When You Grumble Too Much: A Kid's Guide to Overcoming Negativity by Dawn Huebner (Washington, DC: Magination Press, 2006). Read about how to feel happy and more positive.

KidsHealth
www.kidshealth.org/kid
This website for kids can help you learn more about sadness and loneliness, and other stuff about staying healthy, dealing with feelings, and handling medical problems.

A NOTE TO GROWN-UPS

Seeing your child suffer from the painful feelings of being cranky or blue, or from depression or bipolar disorder, can be very upsetting. You know your child is hurting, yet you feel helpless because it seems like nothing you say or do helps. This section offers some practical information and ideas so you can help more effectively.

How Children React When They're Sad

Feeling sad is a normal part of life for children and adults alike. We all experience loss, whether it be through death, moving, divorce, loss of friends, saying good-bye to teachers, and more. Most children will feel sad when these things happen. They may react by isolating themselves, crying, or acting out in anger. With time, however, the sadness fades and it doesn't keep them from having fun, getting along with others, or doing well in school. But for some kids, the sadness lingers. It can affect all areas of their life and sometimes depression can set in.

How to Help Your Child

Give lots of encouragement. Give your child as much encouragement as possible for her attempts to practice the exercises in this book. If she has trouble or feels like giving up, reassure her that with time and practice, you're confident she will eventually learn to overcome her sad feelings.

Let your child know it's okay to express feelings. Many children don't like talking about how they feel. Reassure your child that though it may be hard to talk about strong emotions, the more he does so, the sooner he will start feeling better. Children are sensitive to how adults react when they do share their feelings, so it's important to show you are accepting of those feelings. If you react with alarm or by criticizing, making fun, ignoring, or yelling, your child will stop confiding in you.

Make exercise a family activity. Exercise can help release negative feelings and prevent depression. Ask your child to join you in doing something active, such as a walk, a bike ride, or swimming.

Be patient. If your child is sad or depressed, she may not have the motivation to follow your instructions and may get very angry with even simple requests. Children with bipolar disorder can have meltdowns during which they are incapable of listening to reason. This is a time to be flexible with your expectations. Try to be encouraging but not pushy. Stay calm, try to accept the feelings behind any inappropriate words or actions, and offer ways of expressing feelings more constructively and respectfully.

Observe carefully. Be on the lookout for signs that your child's symptoms are worsening, such as increased irritability, sleep disturbance, social withdrawal, a drop in grades, or an increase in anger outbursts. By catching these problems early, you can work with your child to get the help he needs.

When Is Counseling Needed?

If you and your child try the ideas in this book and nothing seems to work, it's wise to seek professional help. Begin by having your child's pediatrician conduct a full medical checkup. Sometimes there are medical reasons for symptoms of depression or bipolar disorder, and this possibility should be ruled out.

Who Offers Counseling?

Mental health professionals such as psychologists, social workers, and licensed professional counselors can provide therapy for your child, if needed. They can diagnose the problem and decide whether your child's sadness is normal or whether the problem is more serious. Be sure to ask what kind of training and experience the therapist has in working with children with depression. If you aren't sure where to start looking for a therapist, ask the school guidance counselor or a healthcare professional for recommendations. You can also check the phone book under Mental Health Services or Counselors or Psychologists. The list of organizations on page 120 also may be of assistance. Let the agency know if cost is a concern; ask if free or low-cost services are available.

Will Medication Be Necessary?

For more serious forms of depression or bipolar disorder, the therapist may recommend medication. Usually, a child psychiatrist will be consulted who can prescribe and monitor the medication. A child psychiatrist is a medical doctor with specialized training in working with children who are experiencing emotional and behavioral problems.

Before your child is placed on medication, it's wise to insist on a full medical checkup complete with blood work. This way, the doctor can monitor any effects the medicine may have. Bring your child in for regular checkups once a medication has been prescribed.

While medications can be very effective and safe when properly monitored, there can be risks. It's possible that your child may feel worse after taking medication. Some antidepressants, for example, have been linked with an increase in suicidal thoughts in children. Also, it's important to remember that your child may need to change prescriptions, perhaps several times, before finding one that works. Finally, some medicines can be fatal if a child overdoses on them. If your child is suicidal, be sure to lock up these medicines. Ask the doctor or pharmacist about any concerns you have regarding safety, side effects, or other questions.

Don't allow children to be in charge of taking their medication, because if they skip or forget doses the medicine can be less effective. It's important that the medicine is taken exactly as prescribed, and adults are the best people to make sure that happens.

Considering using medication can be scary. You may wonder why medicine is needed, what the benefits are, what the risks are, and whether there are alternatives. One thing to consider is the risk of *not* using medications. For children who are depressed enough to feel suicidal, refusing to consider medication could increase your child's risk of suicide.

Nutritional Approaches

Eating a healthy diet may be especially important when kids are feeling down or depressed. Proper nutrition ensures the brain has all the nutrients it needs to produce the various neurotransmitters and hormones needed for proper brain functioning. Some experts also recommend dietary supplements or vitamins for kids who feel depressed. Talk to your child's doctor to learn more.

Alternative Treatments

When traditional treatments fail, doctors or therapists may recommend other treatments. These may include herbs such as Saint-John's-wort or other "natural" approaches. Some of these treatments have yet to be tested fully in children and some may be controversial in other ways. Be sure to ask about the possible risks and side effects of alternative treatments, and don't hesitate to get a second opinion or say no to the treatment if you're not comfortable with it.

Suicide

The danger of suicide is one that cannot be underestimated. Suicide is one of the leading causes of death among teens and it is a real problem for younger kids as well. In the United States in 2000, suicide was the third-leading cause of death among children ages 10–14. Children as young as five years old have committed suicide. While girls attempt suicide more often, boys are more likely to succeed in killing themselves.

Danger signs include giving away belongings, talking about or threatening suicide, saying that no one cares, avoiding friends and family members, having "accidents" that could lead to death, or engaging in risky or daring behavior.

Always take threats of suicide seriously. If your child seems sad, don't hesitate to ask if he has had thoughts of wanting to hurt or kill himself. It is a myth that talking about suicide will make kids actually commit suicide. Actually, the opposite is true. Seek help immediately if your child admits to having these kinds of thoughts.

You can:

- Call your child's counselor, if he has one. Use the counselor's answering service or emergency number if possible. Having suicidal thoughts is always an emergency. If you don't hear back, call again until you reach someone.

- Contact school officials if your child is in school. Guidance counselors often have training in this area and can refer you and your child if needed.

- Call 911 and have the rescue squad come to your home if you believe the danger is severe. They are trained to deal with mental health emergencies.

- Call the nearest hospital and ask if they have staff who can evaluate a suicidal child or adolescent.

While it's critical you get professional help, there are things you can do to help children get over suicidal feelings. Tell them suicide won't really solve their problems. Many kids think the pain will stop and they'll feel better once they're dead. But dead people don't feel anything at all. Staying alive is the only way they'll ever know what it's like to really solve their problems and feel happy.

It can also help to try to keep children distracted. Sometimes doing something else—like playing a game or hanging out with a friend—can get their mind off their suicidal thoughts. After a bit, the suicidal feeling usually passes.

Some children may need to go to a hospital to keep themselves safe while they get extra help for their sadness and suicidal thoughts. At the hospital, they can talk to a counselor every day. They also will be with other kids who have the same problems with depression. They may have group counseling. Once kids realize they're not alone and other kids understand how they feel, they usually start feeling better. Another benefit to being in a hospital is that doctors can make changes to children's medication faster than if they were not there.

Family members can visit kids while they're in the hospital. Most kids stay about a week, though some may need to stay longer.

■ ■ ■

For more information on parenting children with depression or bipolar disorder, check out the references in the resource section that follows. The better you understand these illnesses, and the different parenting techniques that are often needed to help children who have these illnesses, the more effective your parenting will be.

Remember . . .

While it's hard to see your child struggle with sad feelings and grief, you can provide valuable help. Sadness and grief are normal, yet still require your support. Depression is a very treatable illness. By helping your child learn and practice the exercises in this book, pursuing counseling and medication when needed, and educating yourself about these illnesses, you can help ensure that your child is able to overcome sad feelings and lead a happier, more productive life.

Other Resources and References

Amen, D. G. & Routh, L. C. *Healing Anxiety and Depression* (New York: Berkley Publishing Group, 2004).

Barnard, M. U. *Helping Your Depressed Child* (Oakland, CA: New Harbinger Publications, 2003).

Burns, D. D. *The Feeling Good Handbook* (New York: Plume, 1999).

Cohen, C. *Raise Your Child's Social IQ* (Silver Spring, MD: Advantage Books, 2002).

Copeland, M. E. *The Depression Workbook* (Oakland, CA: New Harbinger Publications, Inc., 2002).

Crist, J. *When Someone You Love Abuses Alcohol or Drugs* (Gretna, LA: Wellness Institute, Inc., 2003).

Dudley, C. D. *Treating Depressed Children* (Oakland, CA: New Harbinger Publications, Inc., 1997).

Fassler, D. G. & Dumas, L. S. *"Help Me, I'm Sad"* (New York: Penguin Books, 1998).

Fristad, M. A. & Goldberg Arnold, J. S. *Raising a Moody Child* (New York: The Guilford Press, 2004).

Greene, R. W. *The Explosive Child* (New York, Perennial Currents, 2001).

Hamil, S. *My Feeling Better Workbook: Help for Kids Who Are Sad and Depressed* (Oakland, CA: Instant Help, 2008).

Hirschmann, J. R. & Zaphiropoulous, L. *Kids, Carrots, and Candy* (Seattle, WA: CreateSpace, 2012).

Kübler-Ross, E. *On Death and Dying* (New York: Simon and Schuster Inc., 1997).

Lynn, G. T. *Survival Strategies for Parenting Children with Bipolar Disorder* (Philadelphia: Jessica Kingsley Publishers, Ltd., 2002).

Murray, B. & Fortinberry, A. *Raising an Optimistic Child* (New York: McGraw-Hill, 2006).

Natenshon, A. H. *When Your Child Has an Eating Disorder* (San Francisco: Jossey-Bass Publishers, 1999).

Papolos, D. & Papolos, J. *The Bipolar Child* (New York: Broadway Books, 2006).

Papolos, J. *Educating and Nurturing the Bipolar Child* DVD. Juvenile Bipolar Research Foundation, 2004. Available at www.jbrf.org.

Riley, D. A. *The Depressed Child* (Lanham, MD: Taylor Trade, 2001).

Rubin, C. *Don't Let Your Kids Kill You: A Guide for Parents of Drug and Alcohol Addicted Children* (Indianapolis, IN: New Century Publishing, 2007).

Seligman, Martin E. P. *The Optimistic Child* (New York: Houghton Mifflin, 2007).

Sood, A. B., Weller, E., & Weller, R. "SSRI's in Children and Adolescents: Where Do We Stand?" *Current Psychiatry*, no. 3 (March 2004): 83–89.

Wilens, T. E. *Straight Talk About Psychiatric Medications for Kids* (New York: The Guilford Press, 2009).

Organizations

American Academy of Child and Adolescent Psychiatry
(202) 966-7300
www.aacap.org

American Association of Suicidology
(202) 237-2280
www.suicidology.org

American Psychiatric Association
1-888-357-7924
www.psych.org

American Psychological Association
1-800-374-2721
www.apa.org

Balanced Mind
(847) 492-8519
www.balancedmind.org

The Bipolar Child
www.bipolarchild.com

Depression and Bipolar Support Alliance
1-800-826-3632
www.dbsalliance.org

International Foundation for Research and Education on Depression
www.ifred.org

Juvenile Bipolar Research Foundation
1-866-333-JBRF (1-866-333-5273)
www.bpchildresearch.org

National Alliance on Mental Illness
1-800-950-6264
www.nami.org

National Association of Social Workers
(202) 408-8600
www.naswdc.org

National Hopeline Network
1-800-SUICIDE (1-800-784-2433)
Provides access to trained telephone counselors 24 hours a day, 7 days a week.

SuicideHotlines.com
www.suicidehotlines.com
This website lists numbers available in individual states.

National Institute of Mental Health
1-866-615-6464
www.nimh.nih.gov

Wrights Law
www.wrightslaw.com
A resource to help you find out what accommodations your child may be entitled to with a diagnosis of depression or bipolar disorder.

Index

About the Author

James J. Crist, Ph.D., CSAC, is a licensed clinical psychologist and a certified substance abuse counselor with the Child and Family Counseling Center in Woodbridge, Virginia. He works with a wide variety of clients, including children, adolescents, adults, couples, and families. He specializes in working with attention disorders, depression, bipolar disorder, anxiety disorders, and drug and alcohol abuse. He is also an adjunct faculty member in the professional counseling program at Argosy University. Dr. Crist is a graduate of Williams College in Massachusetts and the University of North Carolina at Chapel Hill, where he earned his Ph.D. in clinical psychology. This is his fifth book.

Also by James Crist:

What to Do When You're Scared & Worried

A Guide for Kids

128 pp.; 2-color; illust.; softcover; 5³/₈" x 8³/₈"

Mad

How to Deal with Your Anger and Get Respect

160 pp.; 2-color; illust.; softcover; 6" x 8"

Siblings

You're Stuck with Each Other, So Stick Together

by James J. Crist, Ph.D., and Elizabeth Verdick

128 pp.; full-color; illust.; softcover; 5³/₈" x 7"

For pricing information, to place an order, or to request a free catalog, contact:

Free Spirit Publishing Inc.
800.735.7323 • help4kids@freespirit.com • www.freespirit.com